Self-Designing Organizations:

Learning How to Create High Performance

Susan Albers Mohrman
Thomas G. Cummings

Graduate School of Business
The University of Southern California

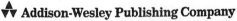
Addison-Wesley Publishing Company
Reading, Massachusetts • Menlo Park, California • New York
Don Mills, Ontario . Wokingham, England • Amsterdam • Bonn
Sydney • Singapore • Tokyo • Madrid • San Juan

Library of Congress Cataloging-in-Publication Data

Mohrman, Susan Albers.
Self-designing organizations: learning how to create high performance / by
Susan Albers Mohrman and Thomas G. Cummings.
p.   cm.
ISBN 0–201–14603–7
1. Organizational change.   2. Organizational effectiveness.
I. Cummings, Thomas G..   II. Title.
HD58.8.M62   1989
658.4—dc20   89-17722
                                                                  CIP

This book is in the Addison-Wesley Series on Organization Development.
Editors: Edgar H. Schein, Richard Beckhard

BCDEFGHIJ–BA–943210

Other Titles in the Organization Development Series:

Developing Organizations: Diagnosis and Action
Paul R. Lawrence and Jay W. Lorsch

Organization Development:
Its Nature, Origins, and Prospects
Warren G. Bennis

Organization Development:
Strategies and Models
Richard Beckhard

Designing Complex Organizations
Jay Galbraith

Feedback and Organization Development:
Using Data-Based Methods
David A. Nadler

Matrix
Stanley M. Davis and Paul Lawrence

Career Dynamics:
Matching Individual and Organizational Needs
Edgar H. Schein

Organizational Dynamics:
Diagnosis and Intervention
John P. Kotter

Work Redesign
J. Richard Hackman and Greg R. Oldham

Pay and Organization Development
Edward E. Lawler

Managing Conflict:
Interpersonal Dialogue and Third-Party Roles
Second Edition
Richard E. Walton

Organization Development: A Normative View
W. Warner Burke

Organizational Transitions:
Managing Complex Change
Second Edition
Richard Beckhard and Reuben T. Harris

Process Consultation, Volume II:
Lessons for Managers and Consultants
Edgar H. Schein

Stream Analysis:
A Powerful Way to Diagnose
and Manage Organizational Change
Jerry I. Porras

Team Building: Issues and Alternatives
Second Edition
William G. Dyer

The Technology Connection:
Strategy and Change in the Information Age
Marc S. Gerstein

Designing Organizations for High Performance
David P. Hanna

Power and Organization Development
Larry E. Greiner and Virginia E. Schein

Process Consultation, Volume I:
Its Role in Organization Development
Second Edition
Edgar H. Schein

Change by Design
Robert R. Blake, Jane Srygley Mouton,
and Anne Adams McCanse

Organization Development in Health Care
R. Wayne Boss

Foreword

The Addison-Wesley Series on Organization Development originated in the late 1960s when a number of us recognized that the rapidly growing field of "OD" was not well understood or well defined. We also recognized that there was no one OD philosophy, and hence one could not at that time write a textbook on the theory and practice of OD, but one could make clear what various practitioners were doing under that label. So the original six books by Beckhard, Bennis, Blake and Mouton, Lawrence and Lorsch, Schein, and Walton launched what has since become a continuing enterprise. The essence of this enterprise was to let different authors speak for themselves instead of trying to summarize under one umbrella what was obviously a rapidly growing and highly diverse field.

By 1981 the series included nineteen titles, having added books by Beckhard and Harris, Cohen and Gadon, Davis, Dyer, Galbraith, Hackman and Oldham, Heenan and Perlmutter, Kotter, Lawler, Nadler, Roeber, Schein, and Steele. This proliferation reflected what had happened to the field of OD. It was growing by leaps and bounds, and it was expanding into all kinds of organizational areas and technologies of intervention. By this time many textbooks existed as well that tried to capture the core concepts of the field, but we felt that diversity and innovation were still the more salient aspects of OD today.

The present series is an attempt both to recapture some basics and to honor the growing diversity. So we have begun a series of revisions of some of the original books and have added a set of new authors or old authors with new content. Our hope is to capture the spirit of inquiry and innovation that has always been the hallmark of organization development and to launch with these books a new wave of insights into the forever tricky problem of how to change and improve organizations.

We are grateful that Addison-Wesley has chosen to continue the series and are also grateful to the many reviewers who have helped us and the authors in the preparation of the current series of books.

Cambridge, Massachusetts   Edgar H. Schein
New York, New York   Richard Beckhard

Preface

Self-Designing Organizations: Learning How to Create High Performance is written to help organizations redesign themselves in order to meet the challenges that confront them in today's environment. Such challenges include the emergence of the global economy with fierce international competition and rapidly unfolding technologies that continually transform the workplace. Unattended, such forces can derail organizations and cause them to flounder and fail. Attending to such fundamental environmental change, in our judgment, requires change in most aspects of the organization.

Creating high performance in the face of relentless environmental change requires an organization to redesign itself so that it is capable of sustaining efficient, high-quality performance through time. The propensity and capability to adapt as performance requirements change must be ingrained in the fiber of the organization. This book describes a process called self-design that organizations and subunits may follow in order to update continually various aspects of their design.

Self-design is neither simple nor quick. Like other design processes it requires skills, knowledge, creativity, and dedicated time. These prerequisites of organizational adaptation must come from organizational members themselves—for only then are the necessary skills and knowledge built into the social system of the organization, enabling it to redesign itself as the environment changes.

The concept of self-design is not original. Karl Weick, for example, wrote about self-designing organizations more than a decade ago (1977). Although there have been several theoretical discussions of the need for self-designing organizations, there has been little *practical* delineation of what it takes for an organization to do it. The process of self-design we describe has been empirically developed by engaging in many action research projects with organizations pursuing self-transformation.

This book targets two primary audiences. The first is line managers, who must know how to lead an organization through the self-design process. The second audience is the change agents—organizational development professionals, consultants, and facilitators—who are resources to organizations that are redesigning themselves. We believe that self-design is the key managerial competence for managing in a turbulent environment. The self-design process will be a fundamental framework for leading organizations and subunits through change just as the problem-solving paradigm has historically been.

The book is organized as follows:

Part I presents the need and rationale for self-design and an overview of the process. The case of the Newtel Corporation tells the story of a self-design process that helped a large regional telephone company respond to the dramatic environmental changes resulting from the break-up of AT&T and the deregulation of the telephone industry. Such massive change in a very large corporation provides the most complex example of self-design. At the same time Newtel Corporation provides a good picture of the kind of dynamic and iterative learning process that must accompany fundamental organizational change.

Part II describes how to lay the foundation for the design process. It provides several case studies that illustrate the building of the three components of the foundation: gaining knowledge, determining values, and diagnosing the organization. Self-design requires gaining knowledge of organizational principles and processes that can guide design decisions, and diagnosing the current functioning of the organization that goes beyond the limited perspective provided by any one person's experience. A clarification of the values that are to guide the design choices is also necessary. The importance of a solid foundation is one of the major findings of the action research projects with which we have been associated.

Part III describes the concept of "zero-sum" designing, in which the design team starts with a blank slate rather than with the constraints of an already existing organization. This approach is contrasted with incremental change or with the imitation of organizational innovations that are used in other settings. Guidelines for designing include the desirability of maximizing the variety of designs that are considered and of minimally specifying the design that is generated.

Part IV describes the action learning sequence of implementing, assessing, and iterating. As is illustrated by the case of the Colorful Paint Company, a great deal of designing occurs after the organization assesses the first changes and finds that more extensive or different modifications are needed. In this rapidly changing world, it is highly unlikely that first attempts will be adequate. The uncertainty is too profound and the required degree of innovation too great.

Part V discusses how to organize for self-design, or, in the terms of Beckhard and Harris (1987), what transition roles and structures are required. Although self-design is more straightforward and easily envisioned in a small organizational unit, it is also applicable in large, complex organizations. One chapter is devoted to the special challenge of self-design that entails large-scale change.

Although self-design may seem unwieldy at first, it is our contention that there are no shortcuts. Like any other capability, successive iterations become much easier and faster. The knowledge and skills that are developed as the foundation is established and as the initial design iteration is generated are useful throughout the successive refinements and adaptation.

We would like to acknowledge the collegial support that we received from a large number of individuals who were colearners in the many companies with which we had the privilege of working. Closer to home, our colleagues at the University of Southern California helped test the usefulness of the self-design model and encouraged us to write this book. In particular, we benefited from joint learning with Ed Lawler, Monty Mohrman, and Gerry Ledford. We also thank the technical staff of the Center for Effective Organizations for their patience through the iterations of this project. Jack Nilles, Annette Yakushi, and Marie Martin were especially helpful when the generation gap between our personal computers caused the temporary loss of the entire manuscript.

Edgar Schein and Richard Beckhard gave a great deal of thoughtful editorial assistance that helped shape this book for the Addison-Wesley Organization Development Series. Thanks to Mary

Fischer and Loren Hilgenhurst Stevens for editorial and production assistance and for being pleasant to work with.

Los Angeles, CA   S.A.M.
                                                                 T.G.C.

Contents

I

Introduction

1

Introduction

One of the most talked about topics in today's business and government communities is organization performance. An unprecedented number of books, articles, and conferences have addressed the performance problems that modern organizations face. They offer a variety of solutions ranging from national industrial policy to specific programs for productivity improvement. There has been a dramatic growth of organizational innovations aimed at improving performance, including job enrichment, quality improvement processes, gainsharing, self-regulating work groups, automation, such as robotics and computerized design systems, joint ventures, and employee involvement programs. Current interest in organization performance is widespread, generating considerable discussion and innovation in both the public and private sectors, in manufacturing and service firms, in smokestack and high-technology industries, and in small and large organizations.

As more and more organizations have embarked on programs to enhance performance, there has been growing realization that designing high-performing organizations is more easily talked about than accomplished. Many organizations have experienced problems implementing the general prescriptions for high performance that are so prevalent in the popular media. They have discovered that performance innovations cannot simply be copied from other successful organizations or written reports. Rather, implementing such innovations requires considerable on-site design and experimentation as organizations learn how to make the innovations suitable to their specific situations (Mohrman and Cummings, 1983). This may involve, for example, setting values to guide the design process, diagnosing the organization to discover areas for improvement, generating relevant innovations, and modifying them as learning occurs. Organizations must understand and be able to carry out these kinds of activities if they are to design themselves for high performance.

This book provides a strategy for helping organizations gain the capacity to self-design their own approaches to high performance rather than rely on external experts and others' innovations. External expertise can provide general guidance for high performance, but organizations themselves must be capable of translating that information into specific innovations suited to their own situations. The book presents steps for carrying out self-design at all levels of organization, from small work groups, to departments and plants, to total organizations. This introductory chapter describes high-performing organizations in terms of the performance demands of today's social, economic, and political environment. General design principles for achieving high performance are reviewed, and a case is made for why organizations need to self-design performance innovations. The chapter ends by outlining the flow of the book.

The Need for High Performance

Modern organizations are facing dramatic new challenges requiring high levels of performance (Mitroff, 1987; Peters, 1987; Waterman, 1987). Utilities, transportation firms, and financial service companies are facing the new demands of a highly competitive, deregulated environment. Manufacturing firms are learning how to compete in a global economy, where there is severe competition from foreign companies with lower wage and raw material costs. Government agencies are receiving public mandates to do more with fewer dollars. Almost all organizations are trying to cope with new technologies, changing workforce demographics and values, and an increasing array of laws and regulations shaping the way they do business and manage themselves.

High-performing organizations are capable of responding to the more complex and stringent demands of today's environment. These demands fall into the following four key areas:

1. Achieving multiple goals.
2. Relating to multiple stakeholders.
3. Managing resources.
4. Adapting to change.

Achieving Multiple Goals

Organizations are increasingly expected to achieve multiple goals simultaneously. They are being asked for high performance in such areas as: financial outcomes; technological and product innovation; quantity and quality of product or service; safety, health, and environmental protection; quality of work life; equal opportunity; and employee rights. Rapid erosion of market share, costly industrial disasters, and lengthy court battles over environmental and employment practices have taught many companies that complacency in any single area is a dangerous posture. Focusing exclusively on financial performance and stockholder return, as American automobile and steel industries have traditionally done, may bring firms dangerously close to extinction.

In today's environment, organizations have little choice but to pursue multiple goals simultaneously, even though they may appear incompatible. Manufacturers have discovered that they must produce products of low cost and high quality. Industrial designers are finding that product designs must be sophisticated yet able to be produced inexpensively and reliably. Defense contractors must seek to optimize the big three—cost, schedule, and quality. Corporate executives are grappling with the fact that stockholders want immediate returns, but that the capital and research investment required for future growth is expanding enormously. Organizations everywhere are trying to be both innovative and efficient.

High-performing organizations *can* achieve multiple goals simultaneously. They have the capacity to organize and focus their resources on a wide range of goals, often discovering innovative ways to reach goals that traditionally seem incompatible. High-performing organizations, for example, can typically achieve high levels of productivity while providing challenging and meaningful forms of work for their members.

Relating to Multiple Stakeholders

Modern organizations are faced with a variety of groups that have an interest in organizational behaviors and outcomes. These stakeholders can and do seek a voice in how organizations operate; for example, employees through unions, due process, and the legal system; customers through individual purchasing power and collectively through consumer organizations; suppliers through customer dependence on receiving quality materials in a timely manner;

managers through hierarchical decision-making processes; owners through financial markets; and the government through laws and regulations. This complex network of stakeholders places a diversity of demands on organizations, presenting formidable pressures on how organizations are run.

Organizations can view stakeholders as adversaries that unnecessarily constrain managerial actions and complicate goal achievement. However, stakeholders can also be powerful allies helping organizations obtain high performance. In turning around Chrysler Corporation, for example, Lee Iaccoca forged a strong coalition among owners, managers, unions, and government who jointly sacrificed for the long-term good of the company (Tichy and Devanna, 1986). Many organizations face similar situations today. They are discovering that achieving cost, quality, and schedule goals requires cooperation among many stakeholders both within and outside the company. The different parties must often give up their past practices and cooperatively develop new approaches for producing high-quality, cost-efficient goods and services.

High-performing organizations are able to form strong alliances with their multiple stakeholders. They have the capacity to respond to the interests of the different parties and to harness their energies and resources for the long-term effectiveness of the organization.

Managing Resources

Organizations prospering in today's environment have learned how to use their resources efficiently. They realize that they can no longer rely on growth to create slack resources, but that they must work smarter with what they have. Companies as diverse as automobile and semiconductor manufacturers have discovered that they can no longer afford to speed up production, scrap a rejected product, and pass the costs on to customers. They can no longer pay high wages as a substitute for meaningful work, nor can they continue to increase the workforce proportionately as the volume of work grows.

A growing number of organizations are heeding the widespread call to "do more with less." They are finding that innovating in today's environment requires a more targeted strategy than the traditional approach of "planting many seeds and hoping that a few grow." They are looking to technological advances in robotics, flexible manufacturing, and information processing to dramatically improve production. Joint ventures, shared investments, and licensing agreements are being used to share financial resources and risks among companies. Organizations are taking steps to increase the psychological and financial involvement of employees, through enriching jobs and sharing productivity gains. Companies are realizing that employees are their most important asset and that prosperity depends on employing human resources effectively.

High-performing organizations are able to manage their human, technological, and financial resources efficiently. They can organize their human and technical resources so that they operate jointly at high levels of performance. They seek the full performance capabilities of their resources, striving to expand the upper bounds of performance.

Adapting to Change

Contemporary organizations are experiencing unprecedented changes in their environment. They are facing a dramatic transition to a global economy, where trade barriers, exchange rates, and international politics can render traditional organizational responses obsolete. They are encountering a labor force with values and demographics far different than those of earlier times. Organizations are finding that technological innovations can wipe out whole industries almost overnight, and that shifts in government regulations, financial markets, and cultural norms can severely strain their adaptive capability. To survive in today's environment, organizations must develop the capacity to influence the environment and to adjust to changing conditions. They must be able to change themselves continually to keep pace with external forces.

Organizations are redesigning themselves at an increasing rate. They are modifying their corporate strategies, work designs, human resource practices, information systems, and structures to better meet the changing demands of today's environment. They are recognizing the need to be flexible and to view organization designs as temporary, fluid structures that are continually undergoing modification and improvement. Organizations are increasingly characterizing organization design as an ongoing process rather than a stable end-state.

High-performing organizations are extremely flexible, continually modifying themselves to improve performance and to adapt to external changes. They are proactive, innovating and changing themselves in anticipation of future conditions. They are rarely satisfied with the status quo and seek to push the "performance envelope" of what is organizationally possible.

Organizing for High Performance

High-performing organizations can respond effectively to the more stringent demands of today's environment. They can achieve multiple goals simultaneously, relate effectively to multiple stakeholders, manage their resources efficiently, and adapt to changing conditions. These performance capabilities enable high-performing organizations to cope with an increasingly complex and uncertain environment, where greater competition and globalization of the economy as well as shifts in workforce characteristics and in financial, legal, and cultural forces have rendered traditional organizational performances ineffective.

These performance capabilities are not easily obtained. The same forces that demand higher performance also introduce factors that make performance more difficult. The government places demands on companies for compliance with EEO and simultaneously introduces costly compliance audits. Employees demand fair and just treatment; their willingness to go to court to achieve it leads to elaborate and costly record-keeping systems as the organization tries to protect itself against the very parties it is trying to treat fairly. The introduction of new technology to facilitate performance often requires upgrading the capabilities of the workforce.

The traditional way to deal with complexity and uncertainty is to allow performance to slip—to build in such costly solutions as buffers, extra resources, and special units to handle environmental change—and to pass the cost on to the customer. Today, organizations must find new approaches that enable them to handle greatly increased complexity, change, and uncertainty and at the same time use fewer resources. This is a tall order, especially for large organizations that have long been set in their ways. Numerous experiments and innovations have aimed at finding the organizational features needed to cope with environmental demands while using resources more efficiently. Although no easy recipes for success have emerged, at least four broad organizing principles for achieving high performance in today's environment can be identified. These include:

1. Multiple information-processing systems.
2. Self-contained units.
3. Flexible structures.
4. High-involvement practices.

Multiple Information-Processing Systems

When faced with highly complex and uncertain environments, organizations need to process considerable information in order to understand external demands and respond to them appropriately (Galbraith, 1977). High-performing organizations are organized to process great amounts of information about their environment and internal functioning. They use that information for two key objectives: to gain closer and quicker contact with the environment, and to integrate organizational subparts, such as departments and work groups, into a coordinated whole.

The formal structure and decision-making processes of the organization channel much of the information-processing activities. High-performing organizations employ multiple systems for gathering relevant information, making appropriate decisions, and communicating the responses to specific groups and departments. They often supplement sophisticated management information systems with less quantitative devices to ensure that information flows in all directions. For example, these include coordinating councils, customer focus groups, employee sensing meetings, cascading information sessions, and weekly videos of "messages from the president." These information-processing systems help organizations better scan their environment and integrate their subparts so they respond to complex and changing conditions cohesively. Furthermore, because the environment constantly changes, organizations will have to continually monitor themselves to ensure that current structures and processes are adequate to perform current information-processing needs.

Self-Contained Units

In addition to multiple information-processing systems, high-performing organizations tend to organize themselves into smaller, relatively self-contained units, such as self-managing work teams and mini-business ventures. Self-containment enables organizations to manage complex and uncertain conditions by forming units to respond to specific segments or aspects of the environment (Cummings, 1978). It decentralizes information processing and decision-making to the subunits, giving them the freedom to respond to immediate conditions.

Self-contained units are not fully independent. They typically operate within well-defined constraints from the larger organization and are interdependent with other groups that may be their "suppliers" or "customers." Self-contained units perform a portion of the overall organizational task, often producing an identifiable product or service. Financial institutions and utilities, for example, often create self-contained business units to deal with different kinds of customers. These units develop specific products or services suited to their customers and often structure themselves according to customer needs. They may also have different personnel practices and reward systems in order to attract and motivate staff qualified to deal with the different kinds of customers.

These first two organizational principles have different impacts. Multiple information-processing systems better integrate the organization. Self-contained units are an approach to breaking the organization into units that can operate differently and effectively without closely integrating across units (Galbraith, 1977). Organizations will have to respond to the challenge of today's environment through a combination of these two approaches. For example, a utility encountering a deregulated environment may find the need to better integrate so that technical changes can be more quickly implemented and service less disrupted during technological transitions. Despite the common technological base, the company may also need to create self-contained business units to interface with different kinds of customers and to develop the services, products, and systems that the customers desire. These self-contained units may be appropriately governed by different personnel practices in order to attract and motivate staff qualified to deal with the different kinds of customers. The utility may end up both more integrated and more differentiated than it was historically. In a wide variety of organizations, the needs for commonality and economies of scale in some aspects of their functioning and for differentiation and responsiveness in others will pose thorny design dilemmas.

Flexible Structures

High-performing organizations employ flexible structures that are continually being modified and improved. They view structures as temporary solutions to current problems and seek to adjust structures to fit changes in strategy, tasks, and environment (Hedberg et al., 1976). Because the emphasis is on organizing, learning, and improving, high-performing organizations encourage employees to question existing structures and to change them if necessary. They ask members to understand their position in the organization through their tasks, skills, and knowledge rather than through the static boxes they occupy on an organization chart.

Many organizations are becoming adept at designing new structures, monitoring their effectiveness, and modifying them if necessary. They have developed a number of flexible structures to perform complex tasks and relate to an uncertain environment. These include research consortia, joint ventures, and other strategic alliances joining firms to perform tasks that are too complex and multifaceted for single organizations to perform or that require more resources than are easily provided by one company. Organizations have increasingly used task forces and interdepartmental teams to share resources and create tighter links among organizational subunits. They have created flexible structures that violate norms of hierarchical control and integrity of organizational boundaries to adapt better to environmental change. Individuals are increasingly being asked to help design and operate within such forms and will have to develop the necessary flexibility to do so. Companies will have to become adept at trying new forms, monitoring their effectiveness, and making changes when they are not working.

High-Involvement Practices

High-performing organizations place a heavy emphasis on human resources, fostering a committed, skilled, and flexible workforce that identifies strongly with the firm's success. They seek a high level of employee involvement in operating and developing the firm (Lawler, 1986). Employees are encouraged to participate in decisions affecting their worklives, and to discover ways to improve the organization's functioning and its products and services.

Organizations have developed a variety of high-involvement practices for promoting employee motivation and commitment. These include enriched and self-managing forms of work design where employees are afforded high levels of task variety, autonomy, and feedback of results; reward systems, such as gainsharing and skill-based pay, where pay is closely tied to performance and people's skill levels; participative goal setting, where managers and employees jointly determine and assess outcomes; employee participation groups, where members contribute to improving product or service quality; and information programs, where employees are given data about the firm's strategic objectives and financial performance. Underlying all of these high-involvement practices is a strong emphasis on training and developing employees. High-performing organizations continually seek to improve the skills, knowledge, and quality of their members' worklives. They use new approaches to human resource management, and they monitor, tailor, and change these approaches as necessary.

The Need for Self-Design

The organizing principles just described provide general prescriptions for the design of high-performing organizations. They identify important organizational features and outline a direction for achieving high performance in today's environment. To implement those principles, however, organizations must learn how to use general knowledge to design specific structures, processes, and practices suited to their situations. They must gain the capacity to self-design their own high-performing innovations (Cummings and Mohrman, 1987; Weisbord, 1987). This enables them to translate the organizing principles into designs that fit the organization's technology, people, and environment. Because these situational features determine the kinds of organizational designs that will be effective, organizations cannot simply copy other organizations' high-performing designs. Organizational structures and practices that achieve success in one situation may be inappropriate in another context. They may need to be modified or tailored to fit another situation, and organizations that can self-design can carry out that tailoring process effectively.

The need to self-design high-performing innovations also arises from the simple fact that existing structures and practices may need to be modified or changed altogether if the circumstances change. Shifts in the environment and technology, for example, can render current organizational features ineffective. Organizations that can self-design are able to respond to those changes quickly, often assessing the situation and modifying organizational designs almost as a matter of course. Indeed, in today's changing environment, self-design may need to become part of the organization's normal functioning. It greatly facilitates organizational change and enables organizations to continually develop and improve their performance capabilities.

As the name implies, self-design is a participative process, involving managers, employees, and other stakeholders if appropriate. Ideally it occurs at all levels in the organization, from top executive teams responsible for the overall strategy and design of the organization to first-line work groups performing particular tasks. The higher level groups provide the context within which lower level units self-design their own part of the organization. The higher level units provide the direction and support for self-design, assuring that lower level units are designing in the same direction while allowing them to develop different designs suited to their different situations.

Self-design is also a dynamic process involving an ongoing cycle of implementing, assessing, and modifying activities. It helps organizations create appropriate structures and practices, continually improve them, and discard them and try new structures if necessary. Self-design is more analogous to erecting movable partitions than to building permanent walls; it is more like pitching a tent on a cross-country trek than building a home for long-term habitation. It rests on the assumption that organizations must have the built-in capacity to change and improve themselves if they are to succeed in today's more complex and uncertain environment. It eschews designing by external experts and encourages organizational members to gain the expertise and knowledge necessary to design, implement, and improve their own situation. The capacity to self-design is fundamental to creating high-performing organizations. It is one of the most critical processes in organizations today.

Overview

This book explains how organizations can self-design themselves for high performance. The material is based on extensive action research projects in organizations seeking to achieve high performance. The firms cover a wide range of industries, including communications, electronics, banking, pharmaceuticals, chemicals, glassmaking, nonferrous forging, weapons, papermaking, education, and county government. In some cases, the entire firm was self-designing; in others, only a subunit such as a plant or department was our client. The authors actively engaged with organizational members in generating and implementing high-performing innovations. We became joint learners in helping members discover how to self-design their own improvements. This involved offering design knowledge, helping to diagnose organizational functioning and assess innovation success, guiding implementation processes, and studying the self-design process itself. This book is the outcome of that learning process.

Chapter 2 presents an overview of a rather complicated case of self-design—a telephone operating company adjusting to its new deregulated environment. Chapter 3 presents an overview of the strategy for self-design and identifies its three major stages.

The next ten chapters describe those phases using information from our organizational experiences. Chapters 4, 5, and 6 are concerned with laying the foundation for self-design by going through the vital processes of learning, determining the values for which the organization is to be designed, and diagnosing the current state of the organization. Chapters 7 and 8 examine the process of designing and offer some helpful guidelines for generating alternative designs to improve the organization, and for choosing a design that optimally meets the needs of the organization. The five chapters in Part IV discuss the action-learning process by which an organization learns through its implementation experiences how to improve its design.

In the final part, Chapters 14 and 15 describe how organizations can organize for self-design, including structures, resources, roles, and norms facilitating the process. The final chapter summarizes the material and draws conclusions about the future of high-performing organizations.

Conclusion

Organizations are increasingly facing complex and uncertain environments. They are experiencing stringent demands for high performance, including the need to achieve multiple objectives simultaneously, to relate to multiple stakeholders, to manage resources efficiently, and to adapt to changing conditions. High-performing organizations have these performance capabilities. They follow a set of organizing principles that facilitate high performance. They employ multiple information-processing systems, create self-contained units, design flexible processes and structures, and promote high-involvement practices. These kinds of high-performing features cannot be copied from other organizations, but need to be self-designed by organizations themselves. Self-design enables organizations to invent new approaches and tailor innovations to their own situations. It provides them with the capacity to implement high-performing innovations, continually improve them, and modify them if circumstances change. The capacity for self-design is fundamental to creating high-performing organizations.

2

Newtel Corporation: Self-Design in Action

This chapter presents a practical introduction to self-design in the form of a case study of the change strategy in action. The case describes how Newtel Corporation, a large telephone company, used self-design to fundamentally change itself in the face of severe competitive pressures and rapid technological and environmental changes brought on by deregulation of the communications industry. We will refer back to this case throughout the book to help ground the conceptual material in concrete experience.

Background

Newtel, a large regional telephone company, was drastically affected by Judge Greene's break-up of AT&T and the deregulation of the communications industry. Even before the nuances of those changes were known, the company set out to formulate a change strategy for dealing with them. Clearly Newtel would have to make significant changes. Emerging from the protection of regulation would require greater market responsiveness and a higher standard of quality service. Costs would have to be decreased rapidly to compete successfully in the new business environment. The company would require heavy involvement from its employees in responding to the barrage of changes that would have to be made in the next decade.

The change task that lay ahead was monumental. Due in part to a recent modernization of its network, Newtel's operating costs were running 20–30% higher than its major competitor operating in the same geographical area. Measures of customer satisfaction indicated a disparity of similar magnitude.

Table 2-1
Newtel Values

Newtel will strive to deliver services of value unsurpassed in the telecommunications industry.

We will respond quickly and creatively to the needs of our customers and to changing conditions in the telecommunications industry.

All Newtel employees will work together to improve continually our business performance.

Newtel is committed to the growth, development, and fair treatment of our employees.

Teamwork and cooperation among all involved parties is fundamental to the vitality and security of Newtel.

Understanding that these changes amounted to a complete transformation of the company, Newtel's executive committee started to formulate a change strategy at an offsite retreat facilitated by external consultants with expertise in self-design. Here the committee spent considerable time and debate clarifying the likely impact of the environmental changes on the firm. It also defined a set of corporate values that would have to prevail if the company was to compete successfully in the new business environment. The values, shown in Table 2-1, would guide how the firm changed itself and operated in the future. The working session was interspersed with educational inputs designed to familiarize the committee with some basic concepts of organizational design and of large-scale organizational change.

The Change Strategy

The executive committee decided to embark on a change process starting with simultaneous thrusts in three areas:

1. Employee involvement in performance improvement.
2. Development of a market orientation.

3. Creation of an information and communication system to keep employees up to date about changes in the environment and new company directions.

Although much could be learned about adapting to the new competitive environment from other companies that had been dealing with competitive pressures for a long time, the executive committee realized that Newtel would have to evolve its own approaches. They would have to be suitable to its unique blend of uniform technology and procedures necessary to operate a worldwide communications network and of market-oriented customization of services that were being demanded by today's customers. In essence, the company would have to design its own organizational changes suited to its specific situation.

The change program was so important that the executive committee decided to serve as a steering committee—mandating and coordinating the work of three cross-sectional design teams that were formed to deal with each of the three identified areas. Each design team was composed of individuals from different organizational functions and levels. The regional head of the union was invited to join the steering committee, and local union officers were appointed as members of the design teams. A key role of the steering committee would be to ensure that the different change efforts were coordinated and linked to the business strategy that would continue to take form as the consequences of Judge Green's ruling became clearer and as the path to deregulation unfolded.

Within weeks after announcing this change strategy to the rest of the organization and after sharing the values that would have to become firmly embedded in the operations of Newtel in the coming months, the steering committee became aware of the magnitude of the resistance that the change efforts would encounter, particularly from managers. Many managers denied there was a problem: "A great deal of progress toward cost-effectiveness has already been accomplished." "Responsiveness to customers is a long-standing strength of the company." "Employees are already very involved and nothing is stopping them from becoming more involved." "There is little that can be done to truly empower lower level employees given the need for centralized decision-making about network and its operating features." And so forth.

Knowing that managers would have to gain a more realistic assessment of the current organization and become more aware of how employees perceived it, the steering committee formed a fourth design team. Its responsibility was to develop an organizational survey that would be used to collect baseline measures about how the organization was currently functioning. These data would stimulate a dialogue in the organization about key change priorities. Periodic administration of the survey in the future would also be helpful in the ongoing assessment of the change efforts.

The change process had barely begun, and it was already clear that a large amount of coordination and information sharing would have to occur among the different efforts. Consequently the steering committee chose a highly regarded manager who was widely believed to be on the fast track to the top of Newtel to be the project head of the change program. He was given direct access to the steering committee and reported to the CEO; he was given latitude to work with external consultants and to develop a group of internal consultants as needed.

The Early Work of the Design Teams

The four design teams started with a combined three-day orientation meeting during which the steering committee shared its thinking about the needed direction, the values, and the rationale for choosing these initial thrusts. Members of the design teams received education about organizational change and a broad overview of the issues and choices that lay ahead. They developed a force field analysis—sharing their thoughts about forces that would facilitate needed changes and those that would block them. This served as a preliminary diagnosis of the organization and its environment. Finally, members broke into their separate design teams and generated a statement of their mandate and preliminary plans for how their team would operate.

During the next six months, each design team learned much more about the area with which they were dealing, visited other companies tackling similar problems, and collected diagnostic data. The communication team quickly identified a primary need—to communicate and get input regarding the steering committee's thinking about the projected impact of deregulation, the company values, and the mandates of the design teams. It developed a process for face-to-face communication and discussion throughout the organization. This effort began to link the rest of the organization to the change process and paved the way for greater employee involvement in it. A number of other communication mechanisms were established for regular updates of employees, including "hot-pink" (highly noticeable) bulletins and Friday afternoon manager open-door periods.

The organizational survey team worked full time for three months developing a survey, testing it with various groups, getting input from the other three design teams, piloting it in the organization, and working out a feedback process that would enable each organizational unit to discuss results and identify areas that it would work on. In the fourth month, the survey was administered, and the data-feedback process began two months later.

The other two design teams having to do with employee involvement and market orientation, respectively, began more slowly—largely because a more complex foundation was required for their efforts. Members spent several months learning much more about their change tasks by reading relevant material and visiting other companies involved in similar efforts. They interviewed focus groups and management teams throughout the company, getting their thoughts about what would have to change and how. They set up a series of lectures during which experienced consultants and people from other companies discussed innovative approaches to employee involvement and market responsiveness. They learned as much as they could in ways that provided maximal exposure to new ideas to others in the organization.

The survey data provided the employee-involvement and market-orientation design teams with additional diagnostic information helpful in identifying areas that would have to change in the organization. By this time, both design teams had identified sets of design criteria—attributes that they would work to establish to achieve greater employee involvement and market responsiveness. At a joint meeting with the steering committee, they shared the criteria and preliminary plans and identified areas that were complementary or contradictory, and where the efforts of the two teams could fuse. At this meeting, concern surfaced that the steering committee was maintaining minimal contact with the change effort, and that many in the organization felt that the steering committee had withdrawn support for the change effort. Because the committee's commitment to change was being questioned, it decided to keep much closer and visible contact with the efforts of the design teams.

The two design teams jointly developed a preliminary blueprint for organizational change, and with the help of the communication team, it was shared and discussed with various groups throughout the company, both in regular staff meetings and in special "town meetings" to which any interested employees were invited. Each meeting was attended by a member of the steering committee and at least one member from each design team. Input and feedback from these meetings were used to help the design teams shape more detailed change plans in their respective areas.

Employee Involvement Changes

The main thrust of the employee-involvement design team was to provide each operating unit with a process and tools to help craft a participative, performance-improvement strategy that made sense given its technology and organization. Operating divisions created cross-sectional committees that were responsible for these local efforts within their respective divisions. This cascading, design-team structure, portrayed in Figure 2-1, was necessary because of the size of the organization and the need to create local champions and accountability. Beginning in operating units that indicated high interest in change, the local design teams were provided with an overview of employee involvement and training in problem-solving, quality improvement, and work-team design. They were given the mandate to begin pilot efforts that were appropriate to their work areas.

To support these local change efforts, managers, technical staff, union officers, and interested employees were provided with training in interpersonal and team skills, communication, problem-solving, and statistical process control. An initial two-day training package was expanded to one week when assessment indicated that two days did not provide sufficient grounding to support the pilot change processes.

A cadre of managers from the operating units was trained to facilitate the changes. Although these positions were intended for high-talent individuals, it was quickly discovered that "surplus" individuals were being placed in them. They did not have the credibility to facilitate change. Consequently a special, two-year facilitator position was created for fast-track managers. They were promised top consideration for promotions and assigned to a mentor

Figure 2-1
Cascading Design Team Structure

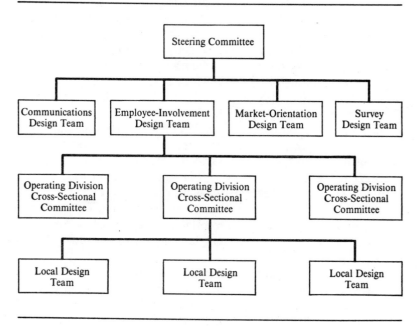

who would be responsible for placing them after the two-year period. These facilitators were responsible for working with local personnel to set up pilot change efforts and to train and facilitate teams. Several facilitators worked closely with sociotechnical systems consultants in work units that felt that work redesign and self-managing teams would be effective. In this way, Newtel developed a cadre of employees knowledgeable about sociotechnical systems design processes.

The divisional, cross-sectional committees kept track of these pilot efforts, responded to requests and problems, and kept the companywide design team informed of how the efforts were going and what additional resources were needed. The communications design team provided assistance in setting up a communication system to encourage knowledge of these efforts and diffusion of the innovative concepts.

Market-Orientation Changes

The market-orientation design team worked in a similar way. After identifying the three primary markets (consumers, small businesses, and large businesses), "overlay" structures were established for each. These matrix-like structures consisted of managers and key technical employees from each function whose cooperation was required to meet customer needs. These business teams were headed by a marketing manager who had formal marketing responsibility for that segment of the business. The job of each business team was to formulate approaches to better meet the needs of the customer, including collecting and disseminating information, setting goals, sponsoring pilot projects, and proposing organizational changes.

The business teams were given training and provided with a skilled facilitator. Their first task was to interview all key stakeholders—including customers and marketing, network, and customer service personnel—in order to discover what customers wanted and what organizational impediments prevented Newtel from delivering it.

Out of these interviews came a series of issues that were shared with the marketing-orientation design team. First, the business planning process was conducted with little customer-related input; it was controlled by the network personnel. It would have to be revised to include multiple stakeholder input. Second, the information system did not provide good information on the cost or service performance of the company vis-à-vis each customer base. The information system would have to be redesigned. Third, the business team managers, who came from marketing, were from the group that historically had had the least organizational influence. The teams would become effective only if appraised and rewarded as business teams. Change efforts were begun in each of these areas.

Modifying the Organizational Changes

This comprehensive change process continued for several years. The initial change efforts each led to a series of adjustments and additional changes. Setting up cross-functional business teams caused other needed changes in the planning process, information systems, and reporting relationships to surface. Those changes in turn revealed the need for team training and for a change in appraisal and development plans. As the company came to better understand its market, two of the business teams were able to further restructure, to set up multiple, smaller self-managing teams that attended to the needs of a segment of the market.

The employee-involvement efforts began with the identification of some hygiene changes that led employees to feel good about the company's willingness to address employee concerns and irritants. On the other hand, these early efforts made management skeptical of the willingness and ability of hourly employees to take performance challenges seriously, and they led to the impression that employee involvement was only for the "hourly." Through an intense assessment process, the design team discovered that, despite widespread publicity and information campaigns, employees were still denying the need for major change. This discovery led to the development of information systems that regularly provided comparative performance data to each work unit so that employees could understand how much they had to improve if the company was to become truly competitive as more and more aspects of the business became deregulated. Supervisors received training on how to manage teams. A few sociotechnical change efforts led to increased interest in work redesign, but they uncovered the need for the union and management to work more closely in identifying contract constraints that needed change, and to ensure that changes were implemented in a way that maintained the integrity of the union and protected employee interests.

Each change was designed only after much discussion with and input from various stakeholders; each was followed by systematic assessment and further modification and refinement. Most changes led to other changes, after the impact of change in one component of the organization's design rippled through and exposed incongruities in other components. Likewise, the need for further change became apparent when changes in the environment, the competition, and the technology of the communications industry continued to develop at breakneck speed.

The communication design team was kept busy sharing information and helping to ensure widespread communication about the changes. The attitude survey became a periodic barometer of organizational functioning and performance and an early warning system about emerging issues, as well as a spur to each organizational unit to take time-out to consider its own functioning.

Downsizing the Company

Perhaps the biggest challenge occurred when the Utility Regulatory Commission served notice that Newtel had to reduce labor costs or have a percentage of them disallowed. This led to a downsizing of the company that was accomplished by a great deal of communication and joint problem-solving. Comparative labor-cost data were provided to all employees. Videos of the Utility Regulatory Commission hearings were made available to interested employees, and the union and management together identified the most likely scenarios showing the vulnerability of the company if all its services became quickly deregulated.

A cross-sectional team from various units within Newtel received training in work restructuring that provided the tools for a redesign process. A work-security policy was jointly developed with the union and management promising retraining and reduction by attrition as a first line of defense against layoffs, and clearly specifying the conditions under which layoffs of both union and management employees would occur.

Results

Throughout the change process, the steering committee met regularly to review the progress of the various change efforts, to ensure compatibility between them, and to initiate major new design efforts when needed. The project manager of the change process returned to a line position after three years and was succeeded by one of the change facilitators who had emerged as a highly respected change agent. The many changes were planned and implemented by multiple stakeholders comprising a large number of design teams at various levels in the organization.

After four years, costs, quality, and customer satisfaction had all improved significantly and were within 10% of competitor levels. Although Newtel still had a long way to go, there was a positive momentum for effective change. Periodic organizational surveys indicated increased trust, highly favorable attitudes toward many aspects of the company, and greater understanding of company goals, values, and strategies.

Continued Change Efforts

Many organizational changes were still underway and had yet to be implemented fully. For example, diagnostic activities indicated that the role of various support groups (human resources, finance, and information systems) had to change to enable operating units to take more initiative. Further change in technology and expanded communication services revealed the need to improve the internal retraining capability. Substantial financial savings and increased profit had led some employees to be skeptical about "What's in it for us?" This led to efforts to redesign the compensation and reward systems of Newtel.

Thus the change process continued at Newtel. Given the fast pace of changes in the telecommunications industry, change would be the rule in the future. Newtel had developed the norms and process of self-design to meet the challenge.

3

Concept of Self-Design

The increased complexity and uncertainty of today's environment have rendered many traditional organizational features obsolete. A growing number of firms are undergoing fundamental change in their structures and management practices to better cope with those conditions. Popular terms such as "reorientation," "renewal," "large-scale change," and "organizational transformation" capture the magnitude of those change efforts, which go well beyond incrementally changing or fine-tuning the organization (Kilmann and Covin, 1988; Mohrman et al., 1989). In many cases, change programs involve significant shifts in the organization's strategy, structure, human resource practices, information systems, and culture. They often involve fundamental changes in organizational members' worldviews and behaviors. Fundamental change can be facilitated if the organization can establish processes of self-design. Through such processes, organizational members can experience the challenges and satisfaction of redesigning their institution, as well as the inherent frustrations and hard work.

Phone companies, such as Newtel, provide a good example of the magnitude of organizational changes needed in today's environment. Deregulated for the first time, they must learn how to operate in a highly competitive situation. Corporate executives need to develop new competitive strategies and the operational plans, objectives, and budgets to accomplish them. They have to restructure the firm to respond more effectively to different types of customers. People must be trained to manage profitability, and perhaps executives must be hired who understand competitive environments and know how to undertake radical organizational change. To reduce costs, the phone company has to downsize—eliminating levels of management, increasing spans of control, and learning how to better use human resources. It must find new ways of operating and doing the same or more work with fewer and fewer people. It may also have to design new information systems, reward practices, and flexible work designs to motivate employees and focus their efforts on appropriate tasks. These kinds of changes require working collaboratively with stakeholders, for example, unions, that were previously considered adversaries. In short, the phone company has to totally redesign itself to compete successfully in its new environment. Fortunately Newtel had top leaders who understood the magnitude of the required transition and provided vision and energy to make it happen.

Although a deregulated environment requires massive changes in how organizations are traditionally designed and managed, similar transformations are needed in many other industries. For example, high-technology firms must implement new kinds of structures and alliances if they are to compete in a high investment, global arena. Firms that survive in the basic industries, for example, automobile and steel, will differ substantially from the bureaucratic monoliths of the past.

The key issue is understanding how organizations can change themselves in such fundamental ways. How can they design or redesign themselves to be successful in an environment with stringent performance demands? The process of self-design is demanding, but it is also exciting. Most important, it describes an organizational capability that can help ensure survival in a turbulent environment.

This chapter first presents an overview of the self-design process. It discusses its background—other conceptualizations of organizational change—and how self-design incorporates or differs from these. It also provides criteria helpful in determining whether the self-design approach is appropriate for an organization.

Background of Self-Design

Self-design is a process for changing the organization design components to achieve high performance. It involves an ongoing series of designing and implementing activities carried out by organizational members (Cummings and Mohrman, 1987). This process helps organizations translate general prescriptions for high performance into specific structures and processes suited to their situations. It enables them to tailor designs that were successful in other organizations to fit their situations. It also helps organizations adjust to changing conditions and continually improve themselves.

The development of self-design derives from two key sources: the requirements for designing organizations in today's environment and learning from other models of organization change.

Requirements for Designing Organizations

The self-design process responds to a number of demands facing organization designers in today's environment. These requirements for successfully changing the design components strongly suggest the need for self-design, in contrast to the more traditional approach of trying to adopt neatly packaged innovations that have been developed elsewhere. Adopting ready-made innovations represents a "freeze-dried" approach to improving organizations, where it is hoped that change will be immediate and produce quick results. Although most organizations prefer the control inherent in a freeze-dried strategy, the following six change requirements point out the folly of this simplistic model of change:

1. Design processes must address the *systemic* nature of organizational change. Organization design components form a system, with changes in one element affecting the others. Because the components need to mutually reinforce high performance, they must be designed as a system of interacting parts. The design of each element must be consistent with the design of the others.

2. The process of designing organizations must be *dynamic* and *iterative*. It must reflect the fact that change is the order of the times and that designing is an ongoing process of adjusting to change and improving the organization. Designing is never totally finished, but it continually seeks to expand the performance capabilities of the organization.

3. Design processes must facilitate *organizational learning*. Innovations for achieving high performance tend to be ill-defined. Organizations must learn by doing, trying out new structures and behaviors, assessing their effectiveness, and modifying them if necessary. Moreover, organizations often start designing with only limited knowledge of design alternatives and vague ideas about what they want their designs to look like. They can gain

clarity about designs by trying to implement them in favored directions and learning from the experience. Such action learning helps organizations to better understand what they really want their designs to be. It also provides a deeper and more realistic understanding of the structures and behaviors needed to implement the designs.

4. The process of designing organizations must attend to *conflicting goals, needs,* and *interests.* Organizations typically include a diversity of hierarchical levels, departments, and stakeholders. Organization design must take into account the different needs and viewpoints of these groups and must seek to reconcile the conflicts among them. For example, it must try to balance the performance needs of the enterprise with the economic and quality-of-worklife needs of employees. It must consider both the possibilities for achieving economies of scale through centralized control and uniformity of practice and the motivational benefits of decentralization and autonomy. The design process ideally helps multiple stakeholders with different goals and assumptions learn together to create a new reality. It must facilitate uncovering and clarifying conflicts among stakeholders and searching for innovative resolutions.

5. Organization design must occur at *multiple levels of the organization.* Top executives are responsible for forging new strategies and ways of relating to the environment. They clarify a vision of where the organization is headed and set values directing how to get there. Middle and lower levels of the organization must put those broad design parameters into operation, creating specific structures and processes needed to implement the strategy. They keep their organization designs up to date, continually adjusting to changes in the environment and larger organization. To integrate the different design levels, designing occurs at multiple levels simultaneously. Although higher levels set clear boundaries for designing at lower levels, the design process must facilitate the negotiation of design parameters and feedback about how the design process is progressing across the different levels.

6. Design processes must enable both *first-* and *second-order change* (Bateson, 1972). First-order change involves fine-tuning existing designs, making them more effective and efficient. It seeks to make designs better, without fundamentally changing them. Second-order change, on the other hand, involves radically altering organization designs. It requires giving up past design assumptions and thinking about design in entirely new ways. Design processes should facilitate both types of change. They must help organizations routinely improve their designs, making minor adjustments as the circumstances demand. They should also help organizations address the need for more fundamental change, particularly when major strategic and environmental shifts are anticipated.

Traditional approaches to changing organizations tend to score low on these requirements for successfully designing today's organizations. They typically include packaged change programs aimed at limited design components. The requirements strongly suggest that such freeze-dried strategies are unlikely to produce significant organizational changes or results. The strategies often ignore the systemic nature of organizations and focus on limited design elements in isolation from the others; they tend to view design as a one-shot event rather than as a dynamic and iterative process; they are frequently designed and implemented by external experts who leave the organization with little instruction about how to improve itself; they tend to focus on limited goals and needs, typically catering to the interests of managers; they often involve limited organizational levels in the change program, usually focusing on either top management or lower level workers; they tend to be concerned with improving existing organizational designs, often neglecting the need to radically transform the organization.

The process of self-design described in this book avoids these pitfalls. It focuses on all of the design elements together, designing them to mutually reinforce high performance. It is a dynamic and iterative process involving ongoing designing, implementing, and assessing activities. Self-design promotes organizational learning by providing members with the skills and knowledge to design their own improvements. It includes multiple stakeholders in the design process, addressing and resolving conflicting goals and needs. Self-design occurs at multiple levels of the organization simultaneously and involves both fine-tuning the organization and fundamentally changing it if necessary.

Learning From Other Change Models

Self-design was developed in the context of current models for changing organizations. A brief review of these frameworks provides a base for understanding how self-design contributes to current change theory.

At least three approaches to planned organizational change are relevant to self-design. The first perspective views organizational change as an innovation-adoption process (Zaltman et al., 1973; Rogers, 1983). It suggests that organizations seek to adopt innovations to reduce performance gaps, which are differences between the firm's current and desired performance. The innovations are seen as well-defined entities or programs that can be adopted by organizations. The relevant literature focuses on ways to enhance the likelihood that innovations will be adopted and implemented effectively. It identifies features of the innovation and of the organization that promote innovation adoption. The innovation literature also describes managerial strategies for introducing change (Kanter, 1983) and organizational processes and conditions that result in the generation of innovations (Pinchot, 1985).

The second framework views organizational change as a transition process (Nadler, 1981; Beckhard and Harris, 1987). It suggests that organizational change involves three temporal states:

1. The organization's present condition.
2. Its desired future state.
3. A transition state where the organization is moving between the present and future.

The transition state must be managed in its own right if the organization is to reach the desired future effectively (Beckhard and Harris, 1987). The literature describes processes for diagnosing present organizational functioning, developing a vision of the future, and managing the transition from the present to the future. It identifies special management structures for the transition process, as well as plans for change activities and for gaining commitment to the changes.

The third approach conceives of organizational change as a learning process (Argyris and Schon, 1978; Argyris et al., 1985). It proposes that organizational behavior is controlled by "theories of action"—members' shared norms, strategies, and assumptions about how the organization functions. Organizational change involves modifying those theories through three types of learning:

1. Learning how to detect and correct operational errors in how theories in action are applied.
2. Learning how to change the norms and assumptions underlying the theories.
3. Learning how to improve the learning process itself.

This perspective identifies organizational features that impede effective learning and develops interventions for improving how organizations learn to change themselves.

Self-design incorporates key aspects of the three change models, but it differs from them in important yet subtle ways. It often entails designing and implementing innovations to improve organization performance, such as computerized information and control systems, skill-based pay, goal-setting processes, employee-involvement teams, and mini-business units. However, implementing specific innovations is not the major goal of self-design. In many cases, innovations will have a short life span, needing to be modified or discarded altogether as conditions change. Thus it is more important for organizations to have the capacity to self-design their own innovations than to be able to adopt specific ones. Self-design enables organizations to generate new strategies, structures, and processes, and to modify them when necessary.

Self-design also involves managing organizational transitions from current to future states. However, this process is more akin to discovery than to planning and managing specific activities to reach a clearly defined end-state. Current knowledge about high-performing organizations is insufficient to completely describe in advance the needed innovations, the change activities to implement them, or their likely impact on the organization. Thus organizations may have only a vague idea of what they want to look like and how to get there. Self-design helps organizations clarify designs through action learning. The transition process involves an ongoing cycle of implementing, assessing, and adjusting activities. Each new cycle of activities results in a clearer understanding of where the organization wants to head and what is required to reach that state.

Self-design is essentially a learning process. It helps organizations learn how to improve themselves, and perhaps more important, learn how to learn. It does not occur in discrete stages with a clear beginning and end. Rather, it is iterative and often discontinuous, changing with the circumstances. Self-design goes beyond the more general models of organizational learning to focus on designing for high performance. It provides organizational members with specific knowledge of high-performing innovations and the skills and information needed to design, implement, and modify them. Self-design is a learning process that never ends; organizations continue to learn more about changing and improving themselves.

The Self-Design Strategy: An Overview

As the name implies, self-design is carried out by organizational members themselves. In practice, there is generally a team, or teams, of designers. In a very small organization or a small unit of a larger organization, all organizational members may constitute the design team. Generally, however, the organization being designed is too large and complex for everyone to be directly involved. Consequently a representative design team that includes various stakeholders in the design process is formed.

Multiple design teams may be required. In Newtel, for example, the design-team structure (illustrated in Figure 2-1) included a company-wide design team, a series of special focus design teams (e.g., Employee Involvement), and a cascading series of design teams that dealt with particular organizational units. (Design-team structure will be further discussed in Chapters 14 and 15.)

Figure 3-1 illustrates the self-design strategy. Conceptually the process is described in three stages, though in practice the stages merge and interact in iterative ways. Each of the stages is briefly introduced in the next section, and the next few chapters of the book describe them in depth with examples from our action research.

Laying the Foundation

When organizations or their subunits begin self-design, they must prepare themselves for activities that differ substantially from daily routines. This preliminary stage provides basic knowledge needed to get started. Without such information, the design process may be ill-informed and superficial.

Figure 3-1.
The Self-Design Strategy

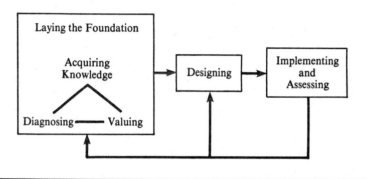

Laying the foundation involves three kinds of activities. The first has to do with *acquiring knowledge* about the basic principles of organization, alternative design approaches and innovations for achieving high performance, and the self-design strategy. This information is typically gained through reading appropriate material, attending in-house workshops, and visiting organizations that are experienced with self-designing for high performance. Although acquiring knowledge occurs early in self-design, it continues throughout the process as participants become more sophisticated and enthusiastic about designing.

The second activity involves *valuing*—clarifying the values and outcomes that the organization is trying to promote through self-design. Values provide the direction for design activities and serve as criteria for choosing and assessing high-performing designs. Valued outcomes are partially determined by the organization's business strategy; however, they go beyond that. Valuing typically includes a statement of principles by which the organization aspires to live. It may also include a vision of what the organization needs to look like in the future.

The third activity for laying the foundation involves *diagnosing* the organization's current functioning. Organizational members usually examine how well the design components are working, as well as various performance measures. This examination provides information about current performance problems and their causes and identifies where design activities need to be focused. It also gives a preliminary assessment of how congruent the organization's functioning is with its values.

Designing

This stage involves generating organization designs and innovations for achieving high performance. Designs are developed to promote the organization's values and to remedy performance problems identified in the initial diagnosis. Attention is directed at specifying key design features and developing a strategy for implementing them.

Implementing and Assessing

This stage involves implementing organization designs. It includes an ongoing cycle of assessing and modifying the designs. Information about how well implementation is progressing and how well the designs are working is collected and subsequently used to clarify design and implementation issues and to make necessary adjustments. The organization continues to assess and modify its designs periodically, learning from its implementation efforts how to make the designs work and how to improve itself. Moreover, the feedback loops shown in Figure 3-1 suggest that implementing and assessing activities may eventually affect subsequent designing, diagnosing, valuing, and acquiring knowledge activities. Through this iterative sequence, the organization learns how to improve its capacity to self-design.

Choosing to Self-Design

Organizations do not naturally turn to self-design when faced with the need for change. Rather, there is a strong tendency to seek packaged change programs—"quick fixes" aimed at solving specific problems. Organizational members need to explore carefully whether such methods should give way to self-design. Self-design is highly applicable (and programmed approaches are highly ineffective) in situations in which:

- Organization design components need to undergo change.
- Forces demanding continual change are likely to persist.
- Learning is required to translate general change prescriptions into specific behaviors, structures, and processes.

- Multiple stakeholders can affect the change process.
- Changes involve multiple levels of the organization.
- Change goes beyond fine-tuning the organization and requires fundamentally transforming it.

When all or some combination of these conditions exist, self-design is a more effective change strategy than traditional, programmed methods. It facilitates the on-site innovation and learning that are required to design organizational components and to implement complex changes. It provides organizations with the built-in capacity to design their own performance innovations and to change and improve the organization continually.

In addition to these situational requirements, an important consideration in choosing self-design is whether the benefits are likely to outweigh the costs. The following benefits can be expected when self-design is performed properly:

- High-quality design decisions deriving from the many and diverse areas of expertise involved in designing the organizational components.

- High commitment to implementing the organizational designs because multiple stakeholders are involved in the process and have a vested interest in its success.

- Enhanced capacity to solve problems, to innovate, and to improve the organization continually because self-design becomes a part of normal organizational functioning.

- High-performance capability, including greater productivity and quality of worklife, greater responsiveness to both internal and external stakeholders, more effective and efficient utilization of resources, and greater adaptability to change.

These multiple benefits need to be weighed against three identifiable costs of self-design. The first cost involves the amount of upfront learning and training needed to gain the capacity to self-design. Those directly involved in the design process need to gain knowledge of the self-design process, of concepts needed to diagnose the organization, and of specific design elements that may need to be changed. This knowledge is generally gained through reading appropriate material, attending workshops and training programs, and visiting organizations having expertise in self-design. In addition to this conceptual knowledge, members may also have to gain behavioral and analytical skills relevant to self-designing. For example, managers may have to learn to lead participatively; participants may need to gain group problem-solving and decision-making skills.

A second cost of self-design concerns the time that it takes to carry out this process. Traditional approaches to organizational improvement tend to focus on specific performance problems and to involve certain programs with clearly defined timeframes. Self-design, on the other hand, is more evolutionary. It is aimed both at enhancing organizational performance and at providing the organization with the built-in capacity to design and implement its own performance innovations as a matter of normal functioning. These dual objectives necessitate involvement by organizational members in gaining design expertise and in carrying out the design activities. Consequently, self-design requires a greater time commitment at the front end of the change process than traditional change approaches. Managers, employees, and staff specialists need to take the time to learn how to perform the design activities. They invest time in the kinds of training activities described earlier, as well as in the change itself.

A third cost of self-design involves the uncertainty of carrying out the strategy. In contrast to programmed approaches to change that tend to include highly prescribed steps, timeframes, and end-states, self-design appears to be a relatively uncertain process. Although participants are guided by shared values about desired organizational performances and designs, the change process involves considerable learning and innovation on site. Members must learn how to diagnose the functioning of their organization or unit and to generate, implement, and assess innovative designs. The precise direction of these activities cannot be specified in advance because the dynamics of the situation will affect how the process actually unfolds. Moreover, because the context of the change program itself is likely to be changing during the design process, members will encounter unanticipated conditions as they self-design. As suggested earlier, many organizations seek the certainty that they believe is inherent in programmed approaches to change. These approaches provide members with the illusion that they are in control, and this can be comforting particularly when undergoing change.

Table 3-1
Benefits and Costs of Self-Design

Benefits	Costs
Quality designs	Upfront learning and training
Commitment to implementation	Time commitments
Enhanced capacity to improve organization	Acknowledged uncertainty
Performance capability	

Table 3-1 summarizes the benefits and costs of self-design. In addressing the tradeoffs between them, organizations must determine whether the long-term, future benefits are likely to exceed the short-term, upfront costs. This can be a difficult decision because it is hard to assess how much initial training, learning, and time must be expended before members can achieve the payoffs from having the internal capacity to change continually and improve the organization. Our experience suggests that organizational members will make the choice to self-design based on their beliefs about how well the strategy fits their values and situation, and whether they believe that ongoing change will characterize their organization. The following case study indicates a situation in which the conditions were ripe for self-design.

Case Study: Long-Life Pharmaceuticals

Long-Life Pharmaceuticals Company was starting up a plant to manufacture surgical devices. The market was extremely competitive, and the plant had to achieve extraordinary performance standards in quality and cost. The decision was made to implement an optimized manufacturing system with a flat structure, self-managing work teams, and skill-based compensation. Every aspect was new to the start-up team—the computerized systems and the new human resource management approaches. In addition, the plant was being built in the Southwest of the United States and would house a workforce different and more diverse than the company had experienced in its largely Midwest operation. Even some of the products were new to the company and used manufacturing processes different than they had experienced in the past.

As far as the start-up team at Long-Life knew, there were no true models for the plant; their particular combination of manufacturing technology, computerized controls, and high-involvement management did not exist elsewhere. A set of visits to a number of other high-involvement plants yielded a general model and some approaches and principles, but almost no direct transferability. Most mature, high-performance plants at that time involved process technologies. The Long-Life staff would have to determine how to apply the relatively general principles of high involvement to their manufacturing and assembly operation. Simultaneously they would be determining how to configure the technical aspects of their production process.

The initial start-up would only be the first challenge—the plant was scheduled for a steady growth for the next six years, as new products and processes would be added. It looked as if the start-up team was going to have to keep discovering and troubleshooting new approaches, and to redesign the plant continually over time. The plant manager and his staff decided to invest a great deal of upfront training time to become masters of the self-design approach.

Long-Life Pharmaceuticals was in a position where the advantages of self-design far outstripped the costs. The new model of management would require a great deal of learning even if it were possible to identify a related plant using a similar model. High-involvement management would entail ongoing learning and the implementation of improvements and changes through time. As the plant came on line and grew through time, it would have to go through a rapid succession of changes. It would have to get buy-in from many stakeholders, develop a workforce that understood that today's structures would rapidly be altered, and make ongoing decisions as to which components of the organization should be set up as self-managing teams and how to integrate across organizational units. Capacity to self-design would be essential.

In truth, a large number of firms face a stream of changes that will extend into the foreseeable future. Rapid technological growth, the unfolding nature of the global economy, and the magnitude of changes required to regain or maintain competitiveness are forces pushing organizations to learn to design their own changes through time. They cannot afford to wait for a well-defined program because such a program would surely be out of date before it could be adopted. Even a "well-defined" program generally requires substantial on-site adaptation and refinement; thus it gives only the illusion of control. Uncertainty will be an unavoidable aspect of the futures of all but the most sheltered organizations. The benefits of developing self-design capability outweigh the costs for most organizations today.

Leadership and Self-Design

Although many organizations need a dynamic, iterative design process, many choose instead to seek the quick fix. Organizational leaders often feel that they do not have the luxury or the patience for an uncertain, iterative change process. They look for a solution that they can decree. This approach may sufficiently alarm employees that they can improve performance through a flurry of activity; nevertheless, long-lasting change is elusive because the organization as a system has not been altered.

Effective leaders of self-design have an understanding of the systemic nature of their organization and know that change involves learning a new way of functioning. They understand their leadership role during transition as one of providing vision, guidance, energy, and encouragement as the organization goes through a learning process. They know that change entails uncertainty and that learning involves trial and error. The organization will only change if the people who populate it are able to go through their own learning processes. These leaders are able to buffer their organization, while it learns, and to communicate the importance of this process to organizational members. They are persistent yet patient.

All of the cases that we describe in this book had leaders who to a greater or lesser extent understood that fundamental change does not occur without a great deal of time-consuming effort. They were convinced that it was necessary to be thorough and to lay a solid foundation for change. They invested their own time and energy in the self-design process, and they modeled the learning process that they desired for the organization. They understood the importance of getting the energies and enthusiasm of organizational member linked to the change effort. Although they were not flawless and certainly not without doubts, they effectively handled the complexity and uncertainty of the change process. Without supportive leadership, self-design would be a very difficult strategy to pull off.

Conclusion

Self-design is a process for helping organizations fundamentally change and improve themselves. It is particularly suited to today's environment, where fundamental change in competitive conditions, technological capability, and the global financial and economic framework challenge organizations to transform themselves radically. Self-design provides a roadmap to help organizations make sense of this potentially threatening process. It enables people to be participants, rather than victims, in redefining the nature of their organization.

The self-design process addresses the systemic nature of organizations, enabling them to change their design components to achieve high performance. Self-design is a straightforward learning process that occurs at multiple levels of the organization. It helps organizations gain the knowledge, skills, and experience to set valued directions, to diagnose themselves, and to generate, implement, and assess innovations. The ability to self-design is essential to transforming organizations in today's complex and uncertain environment. Leading an ongoing self-design process may be the essence of good management in the turbulent times we face.

II

Laying the Foundation

4

Acquiring Knowledge

The importance of acquiring knowledge can be appreciated by thinking about designers of complex machines such as airplanes. None of us would want to fly on an airplane that was designed by people who lacked appropriate knowledge and skills. They must know specific design criteria for choosing among different combinations of weight, distance, speed, cargo and passenger capacity, and fuel efficiency. They must be familiar with the strengths and limitations of alternative aircraft. They must keep pace with technological advances so they can design a plane that surpasses the performance capabilities of existing aircraft.

Although not as precise or well defined, various kinds of knowledge are essential for designing high-performing organizations. Self-designers should become familiar with concepts and frameworks for thinking about organizations and designing them. This chapter addresses two major types of learning that contribute to acquiring such knowledge: conceptual learning about organizational ideas and frameworks, and empirical learning about applications in high-performing organizations.

Conceptual Learning

Acquiring knowledge involves learning about some basic organizational concepts and frameworks. Self-designers need to understand the systemic nature of organizations, including how they interact with their environments and how their various internal components can be designed for high performance.

Open Systems

Figure 4-1 illustrates the basic notion that organizations are open systems designed to achieve certain purposes in particular environ-

Figure 4-1.
The Organization as an Open System

ments (Cummings, 1980). The environment is the source of inputs to the organization or its subunits, including raw materials, information, and demands for specific performances. It also is the ultimate recipient of organizational outputs, such as finished goods and services. The organization thrives to the extent that it relates effectively to its environment by gaining necessary inputs, meeting performance demands, and providing useful outputs. As the environment changes, organizations need to make requisite internal changes to maintain effective relationships and performances. These adaptive changes enable organizations to maintain a fit with their environment.

In today's world, boundaries between organizations and their environment are becoming increasingly blurred. Joint ventures, tight customer-supplier linkages, consortia, and network organizations are trends that result in organizational members working simultaneously in two organizations. Financial interests and records become intertwined, and boundaries become permeable in many ways. Even open systems theory does not capture this fluidity and permeability, which make it impossible to draw a fixed boundary around the organization. Indeed, organizations may use the self-design strategy to develop design features that help them deal with fuzzy boundaries.

Fundamental environmental change requires fundamental organizational change. Many organizations, however, deny this need, even in the face of declining performance. Rather, they seek neat packages and programs to address such issues as quality gaps, customer complaints, and cost overruns. They extol the need to work harder, to eliminate deadwood, and to hold managers accountable, without really making significant changes in how they are designed and managed

Design Components

Fortunately a growing number of companies are realizing that there is no quick or final fix to many of today's performance problems. Poor quality may reflect the way that work is designed, that rewards are distributed, or that goals are set. Deadwood may exist because of long-standing personnel practices, cultural norms, or informal agreements. Current organizational performances result from the interaction among a variety of organizational components that tend to reinforce existing behaviors. Present levels of organizational functioning are locked in by these design elements, making it extremely difficult to improve performance through simple or limited changes.

Figure 4-2 presents a framework, adapted from Galbraith (1977), for thinking about organizational design components. The framework shows two key inputs as influencing organizational design:

1. *Strategy*—The plan of action defining how an organization will use its resources to gain a competitive advantage in the environment. Strategy typically determines the functions the organization will perform, the products or services it will produce, and the markets it will serve.

Figure 4.2
Organization Design Components

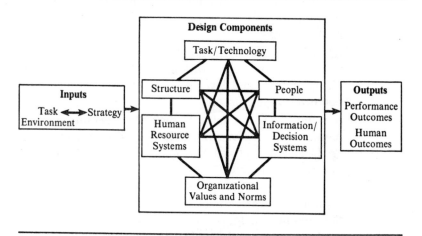

2. *Task Environment*—Those external elements affecting the organization's ability to implement its strategy, including suppliers, customers, competitors, and regulators.

Self-design is typically carried out after the strategy has been formulated when the key elements of the task environment consequently can be known. In a changing environment, the strategy-determination process frequently reveals concerns about the ability of the organization as currently designed to implement the strategy successfully. Newtel, for example, faced a radically altered telecommunications environment that demanded new levels of performance and innovative ways of operating.

Once a strategy is chosen and the task environment determined, organizations must then design their components to facilitate the performance of that plan and to relate to that context (Galbraith and Kazanjian, 1986). At least six major elements comprise organizational designs as shown in Figure 4-2.

1. *Task/Technology*—The activities that organizations perform to transform raw materials into products or services and to relate to their environment.

2. *People*—The individuals working for the organization, including their demographic characteristics, skills, experience, expectations, values, attitudes, and personalities.

3. *Information/Decision Systems*—Those activities aimed at processing information and making decisions, including communication, goal-setting, and feedback measurement processes.

4. *Human Resource Systems*—The practices for integrating people into the organization, including selection and hiring, training and development, performance appraisal and reward systems, and work design.

5. *Structure*—The grouping of task activities into departments and coordinating relationships among those groups, including hierarchy, spans of control, task forces, and special integrating roles.

6. *Organizational Values and Norms*—The shared meanings among organizational members about what is important and how members should behave. They signal how work is to be done and evaluated, and how employees are

to relate to each other and to significant outsiders, such as customers and suppliers. Shared values and norms are expressions of the organization's culture, and they affect the way the other elements are designed. Organizational culture has an overarching influence on all design components and can limit the alternatives considered. Significant redesign may thus only be possible if the change process facilitates a gradual transition to new values and norms. This is a key reason why self-design is so important to fundamental change in organizations. It helps organizational members examine their values and norms and enables them to develop more appropriate ones if necessary.

The lines that connect the design components in Figure 4-2 signify that the elements must fit with one another to achieve high performance. They must be designed to reinforce the kinds of behaviors that are needed to implement the organization's strategy. Traditionally, organizational strategies have required relatively routine behaviors for high performance, and organizations have designed themselves accordingly. Today, however, organizational strategies are increasingly calling for more innovative and flexible behaviors. A growing number of organizations are changing their design components along the four organizing principles identified in Chapter 1: multiple information-processing systems, self-contained units, flexible structures, and high-involvement practices.

Traditional versus Innovative Organizations

Table 4-1 contrasts the design components of traditional organizations with those of more innovative ones. For each approach, the design components fit with each other and mutually reinforce particular behaviors. Both kinds of organizations can be high performing, depending on the strategy and task environment.

Traditional organizations are designed to promote reliability and efficiency. Tasks are relatively routine and certain; employees tend to have moderate to low growth needs and narrow sets of skills; information systems are centralized and closed to widespread access; human resource practices are standardized with routine training, pay based on job occupancy, and narrow, repetitive job designs; structures have tall, rigid hierarchies with functional departments; values and norms promote compliant, routine behaviors. These

Table 4.1
Traditional versus Innovative Organizations

Design Components	Traditional Organizations	Innovative Organizations
Task/Technology	Routine; highly certain	Complex; uncertain
People	Moderate to low growth needs; narrow skills	High growth needs; multi-skilled
Information/Decision Systems	Centralized; closed	Dispersed; open
Human Resource Systems	Standardized selection; routine training; job-based pay; narrow, repetitive jobs	Realistic job previews; continuous training; skill- and performance-based pay; enriched jobs and self-regulating teams
Structure	Tall, rigid hierarchies; functional departments	Flat, flexible hierarchies; self-contained businesses
Organizational Values and Norms	Promote compliance and routine behaviors	Promote involvement, innovation, and cooperation

design features can lead to high performance when the strategy calls for reliable, efficient operations in a relatively stable environment.

Innovative organizations, on the other hand, emphasize experimentation, risk taking, and flexibility. Tasks are complex and highly uncertain; employees tend to have high growth needs and multiple skills; information systems are dispersed throughout the organization and open to divergent sources of data; human resource systems include realistic job previews, continuous training and development, pay based on skills and performance, and enriched and self-regulating forms of work design; structure involves flat, flexible hierarchies with self-contained business units; organizational values and norms promote involvement, innovation, and cooperation. These behaviors produce high performance when strategies demand continuous change and experimentation in complex, rapidly changing environments.

Fundamental organizational changes will likely involve modifications of most if not all of the design components. Changes in strategy or environment generally require corresponding changes in all of the components so they mutually support the new direction. Many firms, such as Newtel, are experiencing this magnitude of change as they try to change strategically from a traditional to an innovative organization. Similarly, changes in one or more of the design elements may need to be accompanied by modifications in the others to bring them back into alignment. Thus organizational changes that are initially limited to one aspect of the organization may rapidly expand to include other features as well. For example, many organizations are currently implementing quality-improvement processes. These programs are sometimes initially viewed as changes in people's skills and knowledge and in performance values. It is assumed that greater awareness and education in quality techniques will lead to radical improvements in quality. Recent research suggests, however, that these quality efforts will have a short life if they are not accompanied by modifications in rewards, information sharing, and work design (Lawler and Mohrman, 1987).

Learning Guides

Our experience suggests that participants differ considerably in their tolerance for conceptual learning. Some may be impatient and want to design without developing concepts beyond those already formulated from experience. Others will seek the security of existing ideas before embarking on a change program. A practical suggestion is to tie concepts and frameworks to specific organizational situations and design tasks. Whenever possible, the information should include practical guidelines and general principles, encouraging participants to apply the material to their own situation.

Conceptual learning seems most effective when given in small doses, allowing participants sufficient time to apply the material and formulate preliminary ideas for improvement. We prefer to teach organizational concepts to members in a workshop setting that facilitates a highly interactive learning experience.

For those organizations that do not know about self-design or have not yet decided to move in that direction, the conceptual learning serves mainly as an introduction to high-performing organizations and the self-design strategy. Attention is directed at describing a wide range of high-performing innovations and explaining why self-design is necessary for creating and implementing them. Typically participants from different organizational levels and departments attend the workshop, and they are encouraged to assess whether self-design seems applicable to their situations.

For organizations starting out on self-design, the workshop combines conceptual inputs with activities for initially developing a design team. For example, team members may discuss their mandate for self-design, decide on operating practices for the team, set norms for members' behaviors, plan diagnostic activities, and schedule future team meetings. Designing their own team for effective performance is a microcosm of the larger organizational design task and an opportunity to practice the values and norms that are selected. Table 4-2 provides a sample agenda of a first-day workshop for a design team just starting out on self-design, and it illustrates the intermingling of conceptual inputs with team process issues.

Empirical Learning

Managers and employees typically are exposed to only a narrow range of organizational designs. Based on their limited experiences, they tend to develop assumptions and resulting design criteria about the way organizations "should be." For example, managers working in large bureaucracies often accept the premise that bosses should earn more money than their subordinates. Similarly many American manufacturing firms assume that those performing work should not

Table 4-2
Sample Agenda: First Day of Design-Team Workshop

I. Developing the Team's Mandate
    A. General manager presents background and need for change
    B. General manager gives team its mandate for self-design
    C. Discussion with team

II. General Organizational Concepts

    A. Organization as open system: external fit
    B. Organization design components: internal fit

Lunch

III. Self-Design Strategy: Overview

    A. Need for self-design
    B. Phases of self-design

IV. Discussion about Operating Practices of Team, e.g., Meeting Time

V. Initial Plans for Valuing and Diagnosing

---

inspect it. In both cases, a growing number of successful firms are operating with quite different assumptions and practices. Unless members learn about plausible alternatives, they will tend to refine and tinker with the status quo rather than seriously change it. Thus participants in self-design must gain knowledge of the range of alternative designs currently being used in successful organizations. They must understand the assumptions underlying those designs, how the designs work, and where they are applicable. They can use this knowledge to reformulate existing design assumptions and to generate alternative innovations for achieving high performance.

Self-designers can gain an empirical understanding of high-performing approaches being used in organizations in at least three ways:

1. Cases and articles.

2. Speakers and conferences.

3. Company visits.

Cases and Articles

Empirical learning can occur through reading cases and articles that describe high-performing applications. Written cases often provide practical depictions of specific innovations and of the change process itself. Review articles tend to cover a broad range of innovations and give examples of the companies using them. The usefulness of cases and articles is limited, however, because they provide only one-way communication. Moreover, they are sometimes written by advocates of the change program who neglect to portray the difficulties of implementing the innovations. Nevertheless, they are a good place to start.

A number of organizations serve as clearinghouses for publications about performance improvement, including the American Productivity and Quality Center, the Department of Labor, University Associates, the Association for Quality and Productivity, and the Center for Effective Organizations at the University of Southern California. A number of recent books provide multiple case descriptions as well as overviews of the kinds of transformations that organizations are undergoing and various innovative practices (e.g., Peters, 1987; Naisbitt and Aburdene, 1985; Kilmann and Covin, 1988; O'Toole, 1985; Tichy and Devanna, 1986; and Mohrman et al., 1989). Other books provide technique-oriented descriptions of high-performing systems (e.g., Hanna, 1988; Weisbord, 1987; Lawler, 1986; Cummings and Huse, 1989; Campbell and Campbell, 1988; and Walton, 1987). Most of these volumes include a rich set of company examples as well as rich reference lists that can help the reader target particular articles and cases from an extensive body of literature that deals with workplace innovation and productivity improvement.

Speakers and Conferences

Designers may also want to attend some of the growing number of conferences focusing on high-performing designs. These include the annual Ecology of Work Conference co-sponsored by the NTL Institute and the OD Network, the HRD Annual Conference of University Associates, regional and national meetings sponsored by the American Productivity and Quality Center, the Association for Quality and Productivity, and the Department of Labor and Federal Mediation Services. In addition, a number of university-based centers such as the Center for Effective Organizations at the University of Southern California and the University of Illinois' Institute of Labor Relations hold periodic conferences where the design of high-performing systems is discussed. These meetings tend to include a mix of practitioners, from consultants and academics to managers and employees. Particular company efforts are sometimes highlighted, and generic issues relative to performance improvement are discussed. The presentations can provide good exposure to concepts, practical advice, and case examples. Designers can develop personal contacts with other companies having experience with high-performing innovations, which may lead to fruitful company visits and information exchanges. The published proceedings from these conferences often provide valuable overview speeches, articles, and reference lists.

A growing number of consultants and academics have worked with organizations in developing high-performing designs. These can be identified through conference attendance, through books and journal articles, and by word of mouth. Having them come and speak to designers can provide relatively rapid exposure to a wide range of innovations as well as to some useful concepts and practical issues associated with implementing them. The design team may want to invite other key members of the organization to such presentations to keep them abreast of new ideas and to promote their receptivity to change. The use of external speakers can also provide good baseline information in planning visits to high-performing sites.

Company Visits

Self-designers can visit other organizations having experience with high-performing designs. These field trips can provide practical examples of high-performing innovations and useful guidelines for designing and implementing them. For example, some U.S. companies have sent designers as far away as Japan in order to see practices and approaches that cause them to question their basic assumptions about designing organizations. Conferences and current literature provide many ideas about companies that have interesting innovative designs.

Keys to the success of these visits include having designers talk to a broad sample of organizational members. This practice increases the chances that visitors will get a realistic assessment of the difficulties of implementing high-performing innovations. Although designers may argue for visiting organizations in industries similar to their own, this may limit the range of innovations experienced and lead designers to believe falsely that they can adopt the innovations without having to refine or change them. A mix of visits to organizations in similar and different industries is desirable. Sending entire design teams to other companies has the advantage of giving all members the same exposure. On the other hand, having subgroups of the design team visit different sites can provide broader exposure to innovations when the subgroups share their "trip reports" with each other.

A variant to visiting other organizations is to invite individuals from high-performing companies to come and share their experience with the design team. This works best if the other organization has a mutual interest in learning about high-performing organizations. A major advantage of having guests share their experience is that the design team can better control the setting for maximal exchange and learning. Also, more members of the host organization can be exposed to new innovations and approaches more economically than having them visit other sites. The primary disadvantage of having guests is that exposure to new ideas and methods is limited to the viewpoints and experiences of the few people who come to visit, often hand-picked and sometimes only indirectly associated with high-performing situations.

Another variant of visiting other companies is to look within the designers' own organization for high-performing innovations and work sites. Large decentralized firms often include a variety of innovations from which to learn. Discovering these novel work practices can provide designers with tangible evidence that their company supports and encourages such innovation. Moreover, it can challenge their often imagined constraints about trying something new in their organization.

Conclusion

Self-designers must develop sufficient conceptual and empirical knowledge about high-performing designs to undertake meaningful organizational change. They may gain this understanding from conversing with consultants, academics, and practioners; from reading books, cases, and review articles; from visiting high-performing sites; and from attending conferences. Some of this learning occurs early in the self-design process. As designers proceed in self-design, they will tend to appreciate the need for such learning and be more receptive to it. Thus, in reality, designers will continue to learn as they go.

5

Valuing

This aspect of laying the foundation for self-design involves clarifying the values that will guide the design process. Values are relatively enduring beliefs about what modes of conduct or end-states are personally and socially preferable. They serve as standards for guiding action and judging progress toward desired ends.

In self-design, values determine which kinds of organizational designs and outcomes are desirable and undesirable. They define what the organization means by high performance. Values provide criteria for judging design choices and the results of self-design. As was illustrated in Chapter 4, successfully implementing high-performing designs often requires major shifts in organizational values and managerial practices.

Clarifying values early in the design process can make these issues explicit and enable designers to become more aware of how existing values may inadvertently constrain design choices. For example, many large corporations have deep-seated values of tight managerial and financial control. These values, and the practices that have been established to foster them, often frustrate avowed efforts to develop more responsive structures required to compete in today's global markets. Similarly, long-standing values differentiating between "managers" and "labor" can thwart efforts to form a partnership among the stakeholders to cope with today's challenges. A large number of symbolic differences and treatment discrepancies such as payroll statuses, perquisites, and physical separation often promote division between the groups at the very time that partnership is being espoused.

Although actual changes in organizational values typically happen later in the self-design process as practices change and people begin to internalize the new values, sensitization to and awareness of desired values should frame and guide the self-design process from the very beginning. An organization that fails to specify its values may design to the "default values" that are already programmed in the system and that have traditionally governed the response to short-term crisis. These values may move the organization in quite a different direction from what might be determined through a conscious valuing process. For example, a default value might be that "labor is expendable"; consequently, layoffs would be the response to a business downturn. An alternative value of organizational commitment to employees and employee commitment to the organization would certainly lead to a different course of action and might result in intensive turnaround efforts on the parts of all employees.

Designers need to address values from at least three perspectives:

1. The performance outcomes deriving from the organization's strategy.
2. The human outcomes relating to employees.
3. The organizational conditions necessary to obtain those outcomes.

Valued Performance Outcomes

Self-designers must understand their organization's strategy or mission and must clarify performance values deriving from it. In many cases, the need to redesign the organization arises from changes in corporate strategy in response to environmental shifts. Designers need to clarify how the organization's performance values have changed if they are to achieve high performance under the new strategy.

Designers may be able to clarify performance values readily if documentation laying out corporate strategy and objectives is available. In other cases, however, designers may need to formulate valued performance outcomes anew. This goal is typically accomplished by creating an organization "mission statement" as part of the overall statement of organizational philosophy. In some cases, the design team cannot proceed until a strategy has been clarified. The case of Model Simulation Systems that follows illustrates the close linkage between the business strategy and values.

Case Study: Model Simulation Systems

Model Simulation Systems is an electronics firm that manufactures sophisticated simulation systems. During its first fifteen years, it grew from a tiny, single-product firm that developed and manufactured simulation training systems as a subcontractor in an airforce fighter program to a medium-sized (1200-person) firm designing a broad assortment of simulation systems. Until 1986, the firm had relied only on financial targets for its strategy and had grown the business opportunistically by bidding on a broad range of RFPs and using its highly skilled engineering workforce to develop whatever technology was required. Increasingly, however, it found itself experiencing cost overruns on its existing programs and being underbid at the proposal stage. Department of Defense purchasing practices had tightened up, and a number of new competitors had entered the scene. To survive in this highly competitive world, Model Simulations would have to focus its new business to avoid the huge investment costs incurred by chasing contracts with such diverse technical requirements. It now had to specify a market and technology niche and design an organization to secure it.

A top-level design team was constituted to redesign the organization to fit the new conditions. It included key managers from various functional areas and several key technologists. This team quickly discovered that the executives had provided insufficient strategic direction within which to design. It was not enough to determine that a concentrated market niche was needed. To design the organization, the team would have to know *which* niche. In a spirited and testy set of interchanges, the design team was able to convince the executive staff that they were sending mixed signals. By specifying only that the organization should be redesigned to pursue a niche, the executive group was keeping its options open to be opportunistic! They were also providing insufficient information for the design team to determine the performance values that should guide the design process.

In a series of off-site meetings, the executive committee and the design team collaboratively hammered out a strategy, in a process that assessed market potential, organizational strengths, and competitive factors. The niche to be pursued was determined by identifying the unique technological strengths of the firm, the areas where past investment gave them the cutting edge process, and the customer base that was most likely to use that technology. The strategy also included financial targets, including booking targets, level of investment, and various economic performance indicators. The design team then felt it had enough context to proceed to the valuing phase of the self-design process.

Several performance values were directly stated in the strategy, and others were strongly implied:

1. Becoming the premiere supplier of simulation systems for the identified military market. (The value is focused market responsiveness.)
2. Being on the leading edge of development of an identified technology. (The value is focused technological development.)
3. Having a rate of return that permitted 6% after tax monies to support new technology advances in the identified technological area. (The value is self-funded R&D.)
4. Developing multiple synergistic programs using common technology. (The value is integrated programs.)
5. Becoming competitive in the production of simulation systems using their well-understood technology in order to fund R&D. (The value is design to production effectiveness.)

By clarifying these value implications of the new strategy, the design team realized that its current focus on broad technology development would be altered during the redesign. This shift would not be comfortable to many people who prided themselves in being on the cutting edge of technology and in being part of the technology development process. A smaller number of Model Simulation's technical workforce would be directly involved in the R&D work. Had the team not gone through this strategy/performance value clarification process, this implication might have been swept under the table and organizational members would have been acting out performance values that did not support the strategy.

Valued Human Outcomes

A second area where designers need to clarify values has to do with the human outcomes of the organization's employees such as work satisfaction, intrinsic motivation, experienced safety and security, and high retention. These outcomes are treated separately here because they are often overlooked; however, human outcomes are very important performance outcomes in and of themselves. Furthermore, they are in part an outgrowth of valued organizational performance outcomes. For example, the strategy of many high-technology firms requires highly skilled professionals to achieve high performance. Attracting and retaining this kind of workforce is thus a key performance outcome having implications for how employees are treated. The organization must promote the human values of growth and autonomy that characterize high-tech professionals.

Model Simulations was faced with a particular problem. Its strategic direction was going to alter the psychological contract of many of its technical employees who had come to the firm expecting to be involved in cutting-edge technology advances and would now be engaged in design rework and less glamorous, "lower status" work. Prior to this point, these "techies" had been satisfied primarily by their job content and their technical opportunities.

The design team knew the company would have to build increased commitment to the business as a business and enable employees to meet their needs for growth and development in a different way—through developing their breadth of knowledge and experience. The new strategy implied a number of new capabilities, including increased expertise in manufacturing, marketing, and business management. As a result, the design team identified the following human values:

1. Growth and development.
2. Business involvement and commitment.

In addition, they built on a number of human values that were the mainstays of the existing people culture and were very important to the various stakeholders who constituted the design team:

1. Job security, which would now depend on an employee's willingness to broaden and continue to develop new capabilities.
2. Respect, dignity, and fair treatment.

Strategic change always carries with it the possibility that the values required to enact the new strategy will conflict with the value preferences of employees. For example, at Model Simulation Systems, engineers and scientists who prided themselves in technology development may no longer find it satisfactory to work in a firm that has commercialization as a primary objective. At Newtel (Chapter 2), long-tenured employees who valued the stability and security of the regulated environment may feel threatened by the new aggressive marketing orientation. There is likely to be a tension, then, between organizational performance values and preferred human outcomes. Ideally this tension can be resolved by creating organizational values that accommodate both; however, strategic adaptation may entail changes in what the organization can offer its people. What is important is that a process be carried out to clarify these issues and make choices and accommodations. At Model Simulations Systems, for example, the team was careful to keep employees fully informed of the strategy, its rationale, and the values that it implied. They planned presentations where employees could engage in a dialogue with top management about what it meant and the problems they anticipated. In this way employees could anticipate the consequences of the new direction for their own careers and begin to make plans.

Valued Organizational Conditions

Self-designers need to address the question: "What kind of organizational conditions are necessary to achieve the desired performance and human outcomes?" Model Simulation Systems identified the following organizational conditions as vital to the achievement of the valued organizational and human outcomes that they had specified:

1. Teamwork among specialists around the needs of customers in the market niche.
2. Employees informed about business results.
3. Information shared about market needs, to enable employees to alter their own activities to better satisfy changing customer demands.
4. Faster design-in-production cycle.
5. Greater teamwork between individuals from different disciplines involved in design-to-production.
6. Continuous organizational improvement.
7. Lateral movement and multi-skilling.

The Value Statement

The product of the valuing process is frequently a written statement of values that designers want to promote through self-design. Typically called a *vision statement, statement of values,* or an *organizational philosophy,* it provides a direction for design activities and criteria for judging their progress. It also provides a powerful means of communicating to organizational members the kinds of behaviors and end-states the designers are trying to maximize. Table 5-1 presents the organizational value statement prepared by the design team from Model Simulation Systems. As we have seen, it represents a great deal of work, not only by the design team itself, but also by the company's executive committee.

Design teams frequently become impatient with clarifying values and push for premature consensus among members. This tends to result in a philosophy statement that is "motherhood and apple pie" in nature. The difference lies in the work that goes into formulating the values and in the extent to which they are related to the organizational strategy, are based on sound organizational principles, and have the commitment of the various stakeholders.

Table 5-1
Model Simulations Systems Values

Organizational Conditions	Human Outcomes	Organizational Outcomes
Teamwork in meeting customer needs	Growth and development	Focused market responsiveness
Employees informed about business results	Business involvement and commitment	Focused technological development
Employee informed about market needs	Job security based on ongoing development	Self-funded research
Fast design-to-production cycle	Respect, dignity, fair treatment	Integrated programs
Teamwork in design-to-production		Design-to-production effectiveness and efficiency

The "motherhood" statement may sound similar to a well-thought out statement, but it is much less useful in guiding the design effort.

Major benefits can be achieved by taking the time and expending the energy necessary to talk through designers' different preferences and interpretations of values and to agree on the kinds of behaviors and outcomes that would be concrete manifestations of them. Because self-design involves multiple stakeholders, underlying value conflicts are likely to exist and must be brought out in the open so members can understand their differences and attempt to resolve them.

Conclusion

The product of valuing is a list of values designers are trying to promote through self-design. Sharing this statement with other organizational members helps them prepare for the organizational design that will emerge and understand its intent. The values also provide explicit criteria for judging members' behaviors so their actions are consistent with the high-performing design.

The process for clarifying values is critical to arriving at a sufficient consensus among designers to proceed with self-design. It generally involves multiple stakeholders, each having preferred outcomes and values. Focusing on the strategy or mission of the organization provides them with a common reference point. However, conflicts and disagreements are likely to emerge as divergent preferences surface. Working through these differences is important because multiple stakeholders will need to support the organizational design if it is to be implemented successfully. Thus the valuing process will likely include conflict resolution when agreement cannot be reached through informal interaction. Most design teams can benefit from having group process consultation from an expert at this time.

6

Diagnosing

Diagnosis is concerned with assessing how the organization or subunit is currently functioning, particularly with respect to the values designers want to promote through self-design. The diagnosis focuses on the desired values and identifies any gaps between the actual and desired organization and any areas where the current organizational design is working against achievement of the valued outcomes.

Diagnosis involves collecting pertinent information, analyzing it, and drawing conclusions about how to design for high performance. It is a necessary prelude to designing the organization because it uncovers those organizational features that need to be changed to maximize designers' values. It also provides a baseline of data against which to assess the impact of the new design. In addition, diagnosis affords an opportunity to get a large number of organizational stakeholders involved in the self-design process.

Diagnosis is guided by conceptual frameworks explaining how organizations function. The frameworks point out what areas to look at and what questions to ask in assessing how the organization or subunit is functioning. Although there is a vast array of concepts and models for diagnosing organizations (Kotter, 1978; Lawler et al., 1980; Porras, 1987), designers can use the conceptual knowledge they acquired in laying the foundation to guide diagnosis. For example, designers of high-involvement organizations may use the framework presented in Chapter 4 that identifies the features of a high-involvement organization to guide the diagnostic process.

This chapter first applies that knowledge to derive a diagnostic checklist of things to look at in diagnosing organizations, and then it presents alternative ways for collecting pertinent information. Finally, it discusses ways to conduct a diagnosis, then feed back results that start to build momentum for change and receptivity to a new design.

Diagnostic Checklist

The framework of organization design components shown in Figure 4-3 can guide self-designers in diagnosing their organization or subunit. It identifies specific inputs, design components, and outputs that can be examined to understand how an organization is currently functioning. Self-designers should be encouraged to supplement the list with other dimensions relevant to their situation or to focus more intently on selected aspects of the list. The major organizational dimensions are described in the following sections with questions illustrating the kinds of questions the design team will want to answer through the diagnostic process. Table 6-1 portrays these questions as a diagnostic checklist.

Table 6-1
Diagnostic Checklist

Inputs

    1. Strategy:

        Is there a well-defined strategy that provides sufficient direction for the design process?

        Is the strategy well known, understood, and believed throughout the organization?

    2. Task Environment:

        What changing aspects of the environment have implications for how the organization is designed?

        Is the organization sufficiently flexible to respond to the rate of change and the complexity in its environment?

Design Components

    1. Task/Technology:

        Are the tools and processes suitable for effective task performance?

        Does the physical layout of the workplace support task accomplishment and coordination?

(continued)

Table 6-1 *(continued)*

Are jobs designed to be motivating?

Is work designed so that people can easily work out interdependencies and process uncertainties?

2. People:

Do people have the technical, professional, and interpersonal skills to do their jobs effectively?

Do the jobs meet the needs and preferences of the employees?

3. Information/Decision systems:

Is information that permits good decision making collected and shared? In a timely manner?

Are decisions being made at the location in the organization that has the best information to make the decision? In a timely manner?

4. Human Resource Systems:

Do the human resource practices select, develop, and reward people for the kinds of performance needed to perform the organization's tasks?

5. Structure:

Do the groupings in the organization provide focus on the key variables in its environment?

Does the structure facilitate the needed coordination and information flow?

6. Organizational Values and Norms:

What values and patterns of behavior prevalent in the organization work against the accomplishment of the performance values that have been established?

Outputs

1. Performance Outcomes:

Is the organization achieving its performance goals?

What are the trends?

2. Human Outcomes:

Is the organization achieving its human objectives?

What are the trends?

Inputs

Two key inputs to organizational functioning are the organization's strategy and task environment. They provide the context within which self-design occurs. It is generally a change in the organizational environment that triggers the need for redesign. Designers need to understand that context and assess whether the organization's design fits with the strategy and environment.

Strategy   As discussed in Chapter 4, strategy is the plan of action defining how an organization or subunit will use its resources to gain a competitive advantage in the environment (Andrews, 1980). It includes the functions the organization will perform, the products or services it will produce, and the markets it will serve. Strategy is also translated into particular objectives or goals that serve as operational definitions of the strategy and criteria for judging its success. The design team will first want to determine whether there is a strategy, and whether it is sufficiently defined to guide the self-design process. These questions need to be answered before the valuing stage can be completed and may be separate from and prior to a more extensive diagnosis. As we saw in the case of Model Simulation Systems, the absence of a well-defined strategy may send the organization back to the strategy-definition stage before values can be set and the diagnosis completed. If the strategy is adequately defined, it is important to know whether it is generally known and understood throughout the organization.

The key diagnostic questions are:

- Is there a well-defined strategy that provides sufficient direction for the design process?
- Is the strategy well known, understood, and believed throughout the organization?

Task Environment   This environment involves those external factors impacting the achievement of organizational goals, including the demands of suppliers, customers, competitors, and regulators. It also includes the wider economic, political, and cultural forces that tend to affect the organization indirectly through their influence on elements directly interacting with the organization. For example, a shift in economic conditions can impact the behaviors of customers, suppliers, and competitors, which in turn can influence how they relate to the organization.

The task environment can be characterized along at least two dimensions that affect how organizations should be designed (Emery and Trist, 1965). The first dimension concerns *complexity* or the number of external elements and their interrelations affecting the organization. The second dimension involves how *dynamic* (changing and uncertain) the external conditions are. As environments become more complex and dynamic, organizations must become more flexible. They must be capable of high levels of information sharing and communication, with less reliance on formal structures and practices and more attention to informal interactions and delegation of authority.

The key diagnostic questions are:

- What changing aspects of the environment have implications for how the organization is designed?
- Is the organization sufficiently flexible to respond to the rate of change and the complexity in its environment?

Design Components

Designers need to assess the degree to which the organizational design components match valued organizational conditions. This task includes determining how well the components respond to the inputs just identified and fit with each other to achieve high performance.

Task/Technology This dimension includes the tools, techniques, and methods for transforming raw materials into finished products or services. It also involves work design or the ways tasks are organized and assigned to jobs or work groups, as well as the physical features of the workplace, such as space configuration, physical ambience, and interior and architectural design.

Two key technological dimensions determine how work and physical features should be designed (Cummings, 1985). The first factor involves *interdependence,* or the degree to which the technology requires coordination among employees to produce an identifiable product or service. When technical interdependence is low, such as would be found in typing tasks, telephone operator services, and reservation systems, the work should be designed for individualized jobs and the physical features should promote effective working alone. When technical interdependence is high, such as would be found on assembly lines and in continuous process manufacturing, the work should be designed for groups of interacting employees and the physical features should facilitate necessary task interaction among team members.

The second technological dimension involves *uncertainty,* or the amount of information processing and decision making that needs to occur during task execution to produce a product or service. When technical uncertainty is low, tasks can be programmed and planned in advance of their performance. Consequently, work can be designed for high levels of external control, including supervision, scheduling, and standardization. When technical uncertainty is high, on the other hand, employees must process information and make decisions on line, and work should be designed for high levels of self-regulation and employee involvement. Physical features need to support either external control by outside forces or employee self-regulation, depending on the technical circumstances.

The key diagnostic questions are:

- Are the tools and processes suitable for effective task performance?

- Does the physical layout of the workplace support task accomplishment and coordination?

- Are jobs designed to be motivating?

- Is work designed so that people can easily work out interdependencies and process uncertainties?

People This design component concerns features of the organization's employees. People differ on a number of dimensions that can affect their reactions to organizational designs, and on their propensity to join and remain with the organization and produce at high levels. One dimension involves people's skills and abilities, which must be sufficient to perform organizational tasks effectively. For example, when there are high levels of technical interdependence and uncertainty, such as would be found in many research and development tasks, employees need to have considerable professional skills as well as the ability to work well together.

A second individual difference concerns people's needs and values. Growth and social needs have been shown to affect how people react to organizational designs (Hackman and Oldham, 1980). People with high social needs are motivated by group forms of work, whereas those with low social needs prefer individualized jobs.

The key diagnostic questions are:

- Do people have the technical, professional, and interpersonal skills to do their jobs effectively?
- Do the jobs meet the needs and preferences of the employees?

Information/Decision Systems This design features involves those systems and procedures that the organization uses to gather information, make appropriate decisions, and communicate the results. Diagnosing these systems involves assessing several dimensions, including the kinds and amount of information gathered and shared, the degree to which decision making is centralized in the managerial hierarchy, and the timeliness and quality of information processing and decision making (Galbraith, 1977). Generally, in situations where the task environment and technology are highly complex and uncertain, information/decision systems need to attend to large amounts of diverse environmental and task information. They should be decentralized so that those closest to the source of uncertainty can process information and make timely decisions. Under simpler, more stable conditions, information/decision systems can attend to less information and be more centralized with slower responses.

The key diagnostic questions are:

- Is information that permits good decision making collected and shared? In a timely manner?
- Are decisions being made at the location in the organization that has the best information to make the decision? In a timely manner?

Human Resource Systems These organizational practices are intended to integrate people into the organization. They include selection and hiring methods, training and development practices, reward systems, goal setting and performance appraisal, and leadership. These practices affect who is hired and retained, and how they will perform their jobs. For example, individually oriented rewards for performance will motivate individual excellence. Team-oriented rewards will motivate teamwork and cooperation.

The key diagnostic question is:

- Do the human resource practices select, develop, and reward people for the kinds of performance needed to perform the organization's tasks?

Structure   This organizational design element involves how labor is divided into groups or departments, and how those separate groups' behaviors are coordinated into an overall organizational response (Mintzberg, 1979). Organizations tend to divide themselves into departments based on functional specialization—products, markets, or a mixture of both—which is called a matrix structure. They coordinate the work of the departments through a number of mechanisms, including hierarchy, joint planning and goal setting, task forces, and special integrating roles. Organizational structure should support effective task performances and environmental relationships. Organic structures have decentralized decision making, flexible work roles, and face-to-face coordination, and they are best suited to highly complex and uncertain situations. More mechanistic structures that rely on hierarchy and rules for coordination, such as are often found in functional organizations, are more effective when tasks and environments are relatively stable.

The key diagnostic questions are:

- Do the groupings in the organization provide focus on the key variables in its environment?
- Does the structure facilitate the needed coordination and information flow?

Organizational Values and Norms   This last design component is concerned with cultural aspects shared by organizational members. It represents taken-for-granted assumptions about what kinds of behaviors are expected and rewarded in the organization (Schein, 1985). Culture tends to focus members' attention on specific organizational goals and behaviors for achieving them. The values and norms of the organization reflect the culture.

Understanding an organization's culture requires examining social manifestations of the shared values, beliefs, and assumptions, which typically appear in stories, rituals, myths, and symbols portraying organizational life. Examining these cultural manifestations can help to uncover deeply held beliefs and values governing organizational behavior. One possible approach to assessing these deep-seated patterns is to ask members to talk about the "rules of the game" in their organization as if they were giving advice to a new recruit. This practice can help separate the culture as it really operates from members' espoused beliefs and values.

The key diagnostic question is:

- What values and patterns of behavior prevalent in the organization work against the accomplishment of the performance values that have been established?

Outputs

Organizational outcomes need to be assessed in terms of designers' values, which serve as the criteria for judging the extent to which the outcomes represent high performance. In general, when the design components support environmental and strategy inputs as well as fit with each other, high levels of performance and human outcomes can be expected. Consequently, diagnosis often starts by assessing outputs. If these outputs are found to be lower than expected, the design components, the inputs, and their interrelationships are diagnosed to discover the sources of the performance problems.

Performance Outcomes This output concerns valued performances resulting from the interaction of the design components. It typically includes productivity measures, such as quantity, quality, costs, and wastage. It also includes financial and market measures, such as return on investment and market share.

The key diagnostic questions are:

- Is the organization achieving its performance goals?
- What are the trends over time?

Human Outcomes This output concerns valued human results of the organization design. It can include a variety of measures, such as job satisfaction, organizational commitment, motivation, growth opportunities, and withdrawal behaviors.

The key diagnostic questions are:

- Is the organization achieving its human objectives?
- What are the trends?

This section has described the general diagnostic questions that can be addressed in the organizational diagnosis. Specific questions depend on the particular values to which the team is designing and on the nature of the organization or organizational unit that is being designed. The next section examines methods for gathering diagnostic data.

Data-Gathering Methods

There are a variety of ways to gather diagnostic data. We will briefly review three major techniques here: unobtrusive measures, interviews, and questionnaires.

Unobtrusive Measures

These measures include company records and archives as well as other data that can be collected without relying on people making judgments. Organizational members often refer to such information as *hard data,* and it is often viewed as the most compelling kind of data concerning the need to change. Trend data is particularly useful in determining whether poor performance figures are a sign of a decrease in organizational performance capabilities or merely a cyclical occurrence.

Unobtrusive measures include records of absenteeism, grievances, productivity, quality, and cost data. Design teams should use such information for diagnosis, particularly in assessing performance and human outcomes. For example, assessing absenteeism and turnover data can tell designers how well the organization or subunit is satisfying employees' needs. Records of customer complaints can help identify performance problems and their sources.

Interviews

Interviews are probably the most widely used technique in self-design for collecting diagnostic information. Self-designers can learn a lot about the organization and environment by interviewing other employees, customers, suppliers, and so on. Indeed, this process is often highly enjoyable for design team members.

Interviews can be rather informal, involving a few open-ended questions, or they can be more standardized, involving a fixed set of predetermined queries. Interviews permit designers to ask people direct questions and to further probe and clarify issues as the interview progresses. This flexibility is important for gaining people's views and feelings about the organization or subunit and for exploring new issues that emerge during the interview. The key drawbacks of interviews are the time demands of gathering and analyzing data and the personal bias inherent in asking and responding to questions.

Ideally members of the design team should share the interviewing tasks, using similar question formats and identifying common themes from the data. The results of interviewing should help focus subsequent design activities on organizational dimensions seen to impede high performance. They may also cause designers to reexamine their values and possibly revise them in light of a frank appraisal of the current functioning of the organization. Indeed, diagnosis often forces self-designers to confront the realities of their situations and to set more realistic values than were initially envisioned.

Although interviewing is time consuming, it establishes a personal link between designers and others in the organization. This relationship can provide designers with access to perceptual information that might be difficult to collect with less personal methods, such as questionnaires. It can also help reduce people's resistance to design changes by assuring that their views and feelings are taken into account in the design process.

In some cases, however, self-designers may not have enough time to conduct interviews, or they may feel that there is insufficient trust in the organization for them to gather valid information. One alternative is to hire outsiders to conduct the interviews and feed back the information in summary form to the design team. Designers should test the results against their own experience and with their own network of organizational contacts to ensure that the information is valid. In one situation where we collected interview data for a design team consisting of managers from different functional units, each member shared the interview findings with his or her respective workgroup and solicited further input about the issues.

Another approach to interviewing is to have designers conduct workshops with a cross-section of organizational members. The workshops are intended to collect qualitative information from multiple stakeholders in an interactive format. As part of the strategic change process at Model Simulations Systems, for example, designers held a one-day workshop with four groups of about fifteen organizational members in each. Working with an internal consultant, members of the design team led workshop participants through a process of uncovering assumptions about how the organization functions, including key operating values. Participants then generated a list of assumptions and values that should govern the organization as it moves in its new strategic direction. Finally, they brainstormed where they felt organizational change would be needed. The outcome of the workshop served as diagnostic input and later was also useful in the design process.

Questionnaires

Another way to collect diagnostic data is through questionnaires or surveys containing fixed-response items about various organizational features. In self-design, questionnaires have two key purposes. They can serve as a diagnostic instrument to help designers gain information on various aspects of their organization or subunit. Because they provide quantitative data, they can also provide a baseline against which to compare organizational functioning when the new design is implemented. For both purposes, questionnaires should be well designed so that results are valid and reliable indicators of organizational features. This goal requires the systematic development of the instrument, typically by analyzing its psychometric properties (Nunnally, 1967).

Many standard instruments exist that designers can use to get at a number of design features (Seashore et al., 1983; Taylor and Bowers, 1972). In addition to standard instruments, designers can develop their own questionnaire tailored to the situation, which has the advantage of assessing features that are highly relevant to the organization. The design team will probably rely on experts to help them ensure that they have a valid instrument and have analyzed the data appropriately.

The administration of the survey may be embedded in an ongoing survey feedback process, or it may be the start of such a process in the organization. Periodic collection of data not only helps monitor progress, it also provides members with feedback that may spur action planning. Wide sharing of the baseline survey data can make organizational members more sensitive to the need for the organization to change and more receptive to the design team's efforts. Thus it is important that an organizational feedback system be designed (Nadler, 1977).

An organization may be tempted to rely solely on questionnaires for diagnostic data because of their efficiency. They can be administered to large numbers of people, and they provide a relatively quick reading of general attitudes and perceptions. The responses can be analyzed rapidly with the use of computers. They have two major disadvantages, however. Questionnaires are impersonal, and if organizational trust is particularly low, people may not be willing to provide honest answers when they are unsure of how the data will be used. People's responses are also limited to the questions asked, and there is little opportunity to probe for more information or to clarify responses. Consequently, we recommend that the use of surveys be complemented with other approaches that yield richer qualitative data.

Building the Momentum for Change

It is obvious that a sound diagnosis is a time-consuming, costly endeavor. The obvious question that a design team may ask is: Since we already know what we think is wrong in the organization, why go through this cumbersome process? The most obvious reason is that the design team may *not* contain the multiple perspectives necessary to truly understand all aspects of the current functioning of the organization. Although they have strong hypotheses, the team needs to test their hypotheses with data that reflect a broader segment of the organization.

Equally important, however, are the roles that the diagnosis plays in promoting readiness for change and in enhancing the capability of the organization to learn. A skillful diagnosis not only includes input from throughout the organization, but it is also fed back in such a way that people become aware of the need to change. If it is guided by the desired organizational values, the diagnostic process can provide information relevant to those values and can actually begin to pull people's attention to those values.

Diagnosis can also begin to establish new norms in the organization. It sets a precedent for examining valid data before acting and for measuring key elements of the organization that go beyond financial and productivity indicators. By drawing attention to these data, organizational leaders can establish the expectation that managers in the system attend to more than their performance numbers; that is, they see themselves as responsible for leading a process to improve their organization as well. Periodic assessments are fundamental to the ongoing learning necessary for the organization to continue to adapt its design through time. Diagnosis, if done well, begins to set in motion the wheels of change and starts to build the learning organization.

The following case study illustrates a very thorough diagnostic process.

Case Study: Imaginative Systems

The Imaginative Systems Company is a firm of approximately one thousand employees, many of whom are software and hardware engineers who design and produce sophisticated imaging systems. After its initial start-up phase, it grew quickly and found itself facing the need for a marked performance increment in business and human outcomes. In growing from a small firm where everyone knew each other and had close contact with one another's work, the firm had instituted many business and human resource practices and a functional organizational structure stressing rationality, efficiency, and control. Quite the opposite of control occurred. Costs increased, morale plummeted, and key technical employees were leaving the firm. Schedules slipped and the design-to-production cycle burgeoned. The firm felt increasingly out of contact with its customers.

The menu of possible problems was long and diverse. To get a sense for the key variables at work, design-team members interviewed a diagonal slice of the organization. They started with group interviews and then held individual interviews with thirty key stakeholders or people judged to be in positions to give particularly insightful analyses of the organization. The interviews were conducted by pairs of design team members. One asked the questions, and the other recorded the information.

The design-team members then pulled out the themes and shared the findings with the whole team. They also shared the themes with the company's executive committee and with several other staff groups in sessions designed to check the plausibility of their interpretations and to solicit reactions from others. A second motivation for these sessions was to begin to get key members of the organization thinking about the need for change.

This process led to some initial hypotheses about which design variables were most strongly related to the company's unsatisfactory performance. The major theme that emerged was that many aspects of the current organization discouraged the close cooperation and information sharing between specialists that was required to design and assemble the complex systems. It also discouraged the customer responsiveness that was required in their heavily competitive environment.

To test these ideas with a larger sample of employees and to get some baseline information about how employees perceived many aspects of the organization, the design-team decided to administer a questionnaire. They worked with a consultant to develop a survey that was administered to all employees. The survey combined some standard scales that had been well tested in many settings with some that were tailored for this firm and the particular issues that it wished to explore.

The survey focused primarily on how well the existing organization—including the structure, the goal-setting, information-sharing, and decision-making processes, and the human resource practices such as reward and appraisal systems—supported teamwork, customer responsiveness, and other performance values. The data confirmed the designers' suspicions that many aspects of the organization were unrelated to key performance values. For instance, human resource and decision-making practices actively discouraged close interaction, especially among professional engineers and scientists in the company.

The design team fed back key survey findings to the entire organization and shared the values and criteria that it would be trying to enhance in generating a new design. It encouraged organizational members to talk to design-team members if they had ideas that might be useful. This feedback process also stimulated discussion in the organization and continued the process of creating understanding that the organization would need to change.

The designers intended to administer parts of the diagnostic survey at regular intervals to assess the effectiveness of the new organizational features that would be designed and implemented.

Sequencing the Activities

We have described the activities for laying the foundation in a logical sequence: acquiring knowledge (Chapter 4), valuing (Chapter 5), and diagnosing (Chapter 6). The ideal relationship among these three processes is shown in Figure 6-1. Acquiring conceptual and empirical knowledge about self-design provides a framework for valuing and for diagnosing. It engenders a felt need to clarify the valued outcomes and organizational conditions for achieving them.

Figure 6-1
Sequence of Activities for Laying the Foundation

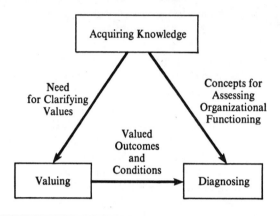

It also provides concepts and ideas about what to look for in diagnosing the current functioning of the organization or subunit to be designed. The values also guide the diagnosis.

In practice, this sequence will not be so neat. Some design teams have little motivation to learn concepts and clarify values until they see diagnostic information indicating organizational problems. Other teams rush to a superficial clarification of values based mainly on personal preference and the popular literature and fads. They eventually discover the need to revise their values to link them more to organizational performance needs.

All three activities for laying the foundation need to occur early in self-design. How long they take to complete depends on how much knowledge about self-design and information about values and organizational functioning is already present in the organization. An experienced design team may only need to acquire specialized knowledge, check the currency of existing value statements, and examine diagnostic indicators already in place. A relatively new design team may need a longer start-up as members with various perspectives and skills develop a common framework and learn to work together at the same time that they are learning, valuing, and diagnosing.

Some new design teams like to charge ahead and immediately start to design a high-performing organization. They invariably discover that there are no shortcuts to self-design, and they need to return and lay the foundation. For example, a problem occurred in early change efforts at Model Simulation Systems. An initial design team was formed based on a superficial diagnosis by top management that the reward system was not motivating employees to contribute the necessary levels of effort to perform successfully on their complex electronic programs. They were looking for a quick fix—a reward system that would rectify this situation. A complex individual incentive program was developed that turned out to be a nightmare to administer and had no impact on organizational performance.

In retrospect, it was clear that top management had misdiagnosed the organization. The major problem was strategic: The organization was trying to operate simultaneously in too many different technological arenas with too few resources, and so people were stretched too thin to meet schedule and cost goals. The design team had not become fully educated about reward systems and had jumped at the opportunity to install a system that held the promise for large bonuses. The system they developed had overlooked a key organizational value—teamwork—that was essential to accomplishing complex electronics projects. They had developed a system that promoted competition between individuals. In Chapter 5, we heard about Model Simulation's subsequent successful use of the self-design process and the thorough foundation that they established.

The quality of the design and the success of its implementation are directly related to the solidness of the foundation that is built. A weak foundation will not provide necessary support for the edifice to be constructed. Eventually the designers may have to tear apart their false starts to build a proper base. They will also have to overcome the organizational skepticism that develops with each abortive change effort. The time and energy required to lay a proper foundation will more than pay for itself during the design and implementation stages.

Leadership is key during this stage. Leaders who push for quick fixes work against the successful design and implementation of change. By being an active part of laying the foundation and encouraging the design team to do it right, the leader can establish a belief in the organization that this change effort is being done correctly and can combat the cynicism that has developed over the years.

Conclusion

Diagnosis involves assessing the current functioning of the organization or unit to discover whether it is operating according to designers' values. Diagnosis is guided by a conceptual framework or checklist specifying what to examine in the organization. The checklist directs attention to particular inputs, design components, and outputs affecting organizational performance. Diagnostic data can be collected through a variety of techniques, including interviews, questionnaires, and unobtrusive measures.

III
Designing

7

Approaches to Designing

Once designers have laid the foundation for self-design, they can begin to design or redesign the organization for high performance. Designing is essentially a creative process of developing something new out of existing ideas, information, and ingenuity (Jantsch, 1975). It is frequently accompanied by mixed emotions. Designers feel excitement about determining the nature of their organization, anxiety about the responsibility of the task, frustration at its ambiguity, and impatience to get on with it.

Because organizations are artifacts created by people, they are the manifestation of designers' values and beliefs about how organizations should be designed. In laying the foundation, self-designers learned that organizational designs are variable and dynamic; they are malleable, not deterministic. Although organizational designs must be responsive to tasks, people, and environments, designing is not an exact process with one correct outcome. Rather, there is considerable choice in designing organizations to achieve high performance. Moreover, as designers learn more about designing, their ability to alter existing designs or generate entirely new ones increases. Thus designing is never really finished, and designs must be written in pencil, erased, and redrawn as time changes. Understanding the evolving nature of organizational design reduces designers' fears of making mistakes.

Designing involves a series of iterative activities as shown in Figure 7-1. It starts with designers identifying criteria against which alternative designs are assessed. Then, they generate a variety of potential designs and test them for consistency among their features and for agreement with the criteria. The results of this evaluation may feed back to affect subsequent criteria identification and design generation. For example, we have worked with design teams that went through this feedback cycle several times. Each time, the team

Figure 7-1
Designing Activities

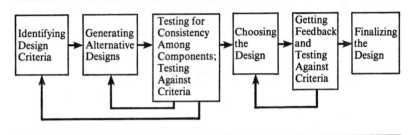

gained greater consensus about criteria, alternative designs, and their assessment. The designs also became fuller and more inclusive and came closer to satisfying the criteria.

As shown in Figure 7-1, once designers have chosen a preferred design, they should undertake one last assessment before finalizing it. This final check identifies whether the design is capable of satisfying the criteria. Because implementing the design generally requires support from others in the organization, it is important for designers to get feedback about the design from relevant others. This feedback keeps the design team from being closed to ideas and promotes understanding of the design in the organization. It may also lead to key modifications of the design that can increase its chances of success.

This chapter describes methods for identifying design criteria and generating alternative designs. Different approaches to designing are discussed.

Identifying Design Criteria

The first step in designing is identifying the criteria that the designs are intended to satisfy. These standards guide designing activities by informing designers of the purposes that the designs are intended to satisfy. The criteria help designers choose from among alternative designs those that are most likely to result in high performance in the organization.

As shown in Figure 7-2, the activities included in laying the foundation for self-design (described in Chapter 4, 5, and 6) provide

Figure 7-2
Identifying Design Criteria

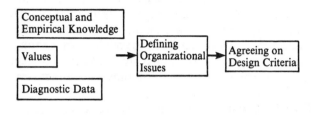

the input for identifying design criteria. The conceptual and empirical knowledge, organizational values, and diagnostic data all help designers formulate particular criteria for assessing alternative designs. Because that input is frequently too general to guide designing, designers may have to translate it into more operational criteria for choosing among designs. Consequently, identifying design criteria is the first step of designing rather than the last stage of laying the foundation. In many cases, for example, designers will generate a large amount of data and knowledge from laying the foundation. They may feel overwhelmed by the enormity of the information and must spend time sorting through it to arrive at a specific set of criteria to guide designing and to test whether or not alternative designs are acceptable. In other cases, designers will be able to formulate specific design criteria when they are laying the foundation, usually when clarifying values or diagnosing the organization. They will have essentially completed this initial stage of designing.

Formulating design criteria generally occurs in two stages, as shown in Figure 7-2. First, designers identify all the organizational issues emerging from laying the foundation. These issues may come from the diagnosis. Designers may have learned, for example, that duplication of effort and ambiguous job responsibilities are causing much frustration and wasted effort in the organization. Issues may also arise from the conceptual and empirical knowledge. Designers may discover that other organizations are improving product quality by maintaining a greater presence in their suppliers' organizations. This may result in the issue of needing to attain greater control over the quality of raw materials to the organization. Designers' values may also be a source of issues. For example, Newtel (Chapter 2) placed a high value on customer service. Although members felt that this value had always predominated, a key issue emerged. The firm's high quality of service had traditionally been in delivering reliable service. Recently, however, customers sought a wider range of services than the company had customarily delivered. The issue for the organization was how to change the notion of customer service from reliability to responsiveness.

Compiling and agreeing on the issues require that designers review the foundation that they have established and pull out all the major themes and concerns that have emerged. A useful approach is a nominal group process in which each individual, perhaps in preparation for a design team meeting, reviews the materials and identifies issues that are important (Delbecq et al., 1975). The lists can then be shared, discussed, and synthesized through group discussion. The added benefit of this activity is that the team has a chance to take stock of where it is in the self-design process and what it has accomplished. It also serves as a review and a bridge between laying the foundation and designing. We have seen design teams lay a strong foundation and then fail to apply it to the designing process.

Once organizational issues have been identified, designers must derive specific design criteria from them. This process includes prioritizing the issues and then stating them as standards that are sufficiently concrete to judge alternative designs. For example, one design criterion identified by the design team in Model Simulation Systems (Chapter 5) was: "The organization will have methods for regularly assessing customer needs and getting all functions involved in developing and delivering appropriate services." This criterion guided the designing process and helped designers evaluate alternative proposals.

For some design teams, identifying design criteria will seem like revisiting old ideas from laying the foundation. Although designers may feel that these criteria have already been formulated, they should test this assumption. Testing will provide a final check that designers' different assumptions and values have been thoroughly discussed and a sufficient consensus has been achieved about specific standards for guiding the remaining stages of self-design. The following case study illustrates the process of determining design criteria.

Case Study: Hi-Value Human Resources

The Hi-Value Company was facing a number of strategic challenges that had significant human resource implications. The company relied on its excellent technical staff to produce a steady stream of new products for its multiple businesses, and on its financial and marketing staffs for rapid commercialization. Increasingly the complexity and costs of technical development were placing heavy demands for cost control in the product development process. The marketplace was demanding cost competitiveness from a company that had always relied on product innovation to stay ahead of its competitors and that had come to rely on the sizable margins that it could attain by being the first to the market. Hi-Value was facing the challenges of innovating with an aging workforce, dealing with increasing workforce diversity, and finding new approaches to motivating employees despite decreasing promotional opportunities. Furthermore, its various businesses were encountering increasingly diverse environments, causing them to question the appropriateness of uniform human resource policies and practices.

The human resource function embarked on a self-design process. They recognized that they were working within a context where shifts in corporate strategy were affecting the mission of their unit and the values they had to foster. Although new product innovation would remain the life-blood of the company, cost effectiveness would assume increasing importance. Furthermore, the establishment of corporate strategic business groups was indicative of an increasing value being placed on allowing each business group to adapt to its own market. This procedure had implications for not only the nature of the human resource services they delivered in the corporation, but also for the design of the Human Resources organization.

The design team collected diagnostic information from customers (other units in the organization) and from a cross-section of human resource employees. Customers were increasingly looking to human resources to help them solve complex problems such as workforce obsolescence, and motivating a mature workforce in a flat organization structure. The line organizations found it cumbersome to deal with the various corporate human resource functions (e.g., compensation, staffing, and human resources development) as if they were separate organizations. They wanted to be able to interface with one human resource generalist who could "broker" and coordinate the various human resource functions and services. Line managers questioned the skill level of human resource employees.

The internal diagnosis found human resource employees feeling overburdened with paperwork and compliance enforcement activities. They felt that many line managers relied on them to manage their people problems and that a great deal of their time was taken tending to problems that these managers had caused by poor people management practices. They were frustrated by their lack of time and skills to address the important problems their line organizations faced. Human resource representatives, who serviced the line organizations, felt that human resource policies were inflexibly controlled by corporate staff groups, leading them to always be in the position of denying requests for deviation that they received from their line customers. Furthermore, human resource employees felt that the department was insensitive to their own needs for development and career enhancement.

The design team spent a great deal of time agreeing on the design criteria. The difficulty was that not all members agreed with the values that were implied by the corporate strategy—particularly

Table 7-1
Examples of Design Criteria From the Hi-Value Human Resources Function

---

The new design will be tested against its ability to:
1. Place accountability for people management in the line organization.
2. Be responsive to the particular needs of the various businesses.
3. Focus multiple human resource disciplines on complex problems.
4. Provide cost-effective services.
5. Provide career paths and multidisciplinary competence development for human resource professionals.
6. Reduce paperwork transactions.
7. Maintain the long-standing corporate values of respect and fair treatment for all employees.

---

the move away from uniformity and toward more business specific adaptation. After much discussion and review of the issues that emerged from the valuing process and from the internal and external diagnoses, the team agreed on the list of criteria in Table 7-1. This list would be invaluable throughout the design process since several design team members were personally uncomfortable with several of the implied directions. These members were able to agree about the necessity to move in this direction, but unable to shift their own personal value system, which was more comfortable with uniformity and centralized control. The criteria became a quick reference point at times during the design process when it was clear that members of the design team were working at cross purposes.

Because the human resource department was self-designing within a larger corporate context, it was important for it to test these criteria with key stakeholders. They were shared with the executive group of the company and with other key customer stakeholders to determine whether or not there were unforeseen problems or resistances to this direction. They received favorable response, which reinforced their general direction. The design team also shared this list of criteria with human resource employees as a way to link them to their efforts and in a format that enabled them to elicit input that would be useful in the actual designing process.

Generating Alternative Designs

Once design criteria have been identified, designers can generate alternative designs to satisfy the standards. Figure 7-3 identifies three major approaches to generating alternative designs, depending

Figure 7-3
Approaches to Designing

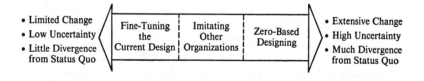

on the extensiveness of the changes envisioned, the amount of uncertainty involved in implementing them, and the degree to which they depart from the status quo. The simplest approach involves fine-tuning an existing organizational design. It includes limited organizational changes, a good deal of certainty in implementation, and minimal departure from the status quo. A more complex approach involves imitating other organizations' designs. The most complex method is zero-based designing, which involves creating an entirely new organization from scratch. It includes extensive organizational changes, considerable uncertainty, and transformation of the status quo.

Fine-Tuning the Current Design

This approach to designing consists of modifying the existing organizational design to improve it. It involves making incremental changes within the organization's current frame of reference. Designers do not have to change their fundamental assumptions about how organizations work or install a new logic to organizational operations. Rather, they can design within the constraints of the organization as they know and understand it, which results in *first-order change* aimed at making better what is already there (Argyris and Schon, 1978). Design teams following this approach use diagnostic information to identify areas where improvement is desirable. They engage in a process similar to traditional problem-solving.

Designers tend to use fine-tuning when they believe that the current organizational design is basically sound yet could be improved. In laying the foundation, designers may discover that the existing design meets technological and human needs and satisfies most of the designers' values. Small changes and tinkering can improve performance in these areas without the need for fundamental change. Diagnosis in an electronics plant revealed that the people were motivated, interested in their work, and felt that the current design enabled good task performance. However, large amounts of rework were costing the firm a great deal. The design team discovered that the major cause of this problem was the operators' misinterpretation of manually written product specifications, which resulted in production that was out of specification. They designed an electronic process for entering and tracking product specifications, dramatically reducing the rework problem. The designers concluded that extensive organizational change was unnecessary at that time.

Some organizations have tended to use fine-tuning as a "quick fix" for problems requiring more fundamental change (Kilmann, 1984). They try to solve performance problems without investing the time or resources needed to improve the situation. A small manufacturing firm was experiencing high turnover, low morale, and unacceptable costs. Diagnosis showed that employees felt stagnant and apathetic with little pride in their work. Management was highly autocratic, and there was little cooperation across functional units. Although this situation was clearly a case for major redesign, top management decided to implement a quality-awareness program to sensitize employees about their crucial part in producing quality products. The rationale for the program was that managers could not be spared the time to redesign the firm but were needed full time to solve problems in the chaotic, firefighting environment. Top management was looking for a magical solution to problems requiring extensive organizational change.

Imitating Other Organizations

A second approach to designing is to imitate designs that have been successful in other organizations. In laying the foundation, designers may become aware of innovations in other organizations that seem suited to their own situation. These innovations may appear to address the problems discovered in diagnosis or to promote designers' values. They may embody a new logic of organizational functioning. For example, a design team may decide to imitate another organization's gainsharing program. The team may reproduce the basic features of this innovation, including a formula for distributing productivity gains, employee suggestion committees, and a pool of implementation funds to help make initial cost-saving improvements suggested by employees. The design team may need to tailor each of these features to fit its situation. The notion of sharing gains with employees and giving them the time, information, and resources to suggest and implement improvements may constitute a significant change. Imitating the design of other organizations permits designers to engage in vicarious learning. It may lessen the risk of innovation and shorten the designing period.

Imitation can be dangerous, however. Designers may misjudge the applicability of the innovation to their own situation. Their vicarious learning may be incomplete, resulting in erroneous understanding of what is needed for the design's success. A construction firm imitated all aspects of another firm's gainsharing program except one—the training of management in participative skills. The company reasoned that because its managers were well experienced and liked, they would not need the time-consuming training. The firm had little success with the gainsharing program because managers did not assist in implementing employee ideas and suggestions, nor did they believe it was their role to do so. The technical aspects of gainsharing had been imitated accurately, but a key design feature had been eliminated. Thus designers wishing to imitate others' innovations should take great care to understand and implement the design features necessary for success.

Another problem with imitating others' innovations is that designers tend to focus on the innovations while neglecting other aspects of the organization that may need to be changed to support them. This problem occurred in many companies trying to implement quality circles in the early 1980s (Lawler and Mohrman, 1985). They often tried to imitate the circles programs of other organizations without realizing that other design components, such as management style, information systems, and reward practices, had to be modified to support the participative thrust of the program. Indeed, consultants frequently sold quality circles as an innovation that leaves the rest of the organization unchanged. The quality circles programs had limited success in many organizations because designers did not learn a new way to think about the responsibilities of employees and managers. Consequently, they failed to make the requisite changes in reward practices, information systems, and leadership styles needed to provide a fertile context for quality circles.

Zero-Based Designing

This third approach to designing involves fundamentally changing the organization or subunit, often starting with a blank sheet of paper and ignoring the constraints of the current design. We have called this zero-based designing to emphasize that it goes well beyond fine-tuning the status quo to designing an entirely new organization from scratch. This practice results in *second-order change* aimed at altering the assumptions and values underlying existing organizational designs (Argyris and Schon, 1978).

Zero-based designing can evoke considerable anxiety in designers, particularly when they do not see the need for fundamental change or believe they have the skills required for it. Of the three approaches to designing, the zero-based method is by far the most creative. Consequently, it will not be equally appealing to all designers. Designing in this manner itself constitutes novel action for most people. The logic of most organizations demands conformity and provides the security of well-known standards and practices. Designing from scratch provides freedom from existing constraints, yet results in the insecurity inherent in any truly creative act (McWhinney, 1980).

Zero-based designing demands a thorough foundation in self-design. Designers must appreciate the need for such change and have the conceptual knowledge and commitment to values needed to design it. Zero-based designing is both instrumental and expressive. It is intended to accomplish certain outcomes and embodies the values and aesthetics of the designers.

This design approach includes creative moments when conceptual breakthroughs of new organizational designs occur. It also involves large doses of systematically engineering the various design components to support the concepts. Self-designers in Model Simulations Systems (Chapter 5) set out in a fairly routine manner to redesign their organization to support a new customer-driven strategy. Much of their activity consisted of discussing such questions as: If we want to be customer driven, who should interface with the customer? Answering this kind of question was relatively mechanical once designers accepted the notion that customer contact (rather than expert technical knowledge) was the prime source of information about customer needs. However, the process was more animated when designers examined how to establish teamwork among specialists in the company. Here they had a conceptual breakthrough. They conceived of an organization comprised of a hierarchy of interdisciplinary teams. Members of a technical team would continue to have a "boss" in their functional area, but the team as a whole would report into a higher level interdisciplinary team. The higher level team would be the appeals court for matters such as priority determination or capital expenditure that were beyond the authority of the project team. It would also determine rewards for the project team and make personnel decisions. Thus interdisciplinary perspectives would inform all key decisions.

Another conceptual breakthrough occurred when discussing the value of technical excellence. Designers wanted to create an organization where it is possible to remain technically state-of-the-art while becoming knowledgeable about business aspects of projects and advancing organizationally. They developed a concept of fluid movement within the organization, permitting an individual to move between managerial responsibilities on one project and technical contributions on another without changing pay grades or job classifications. An individual capable of making both kinds of contributions who actually contributed in both ways would be classified at a higher grade level because of the breadth and flexibility of his or her contribution. Both of these conceptual breakthroughs constituted a fundamental change in the status quo. They became keystones in designing the new organization, enabling designers to engineer systematically other features to support the novel concepts.

All designing tends to be limited by what is familiar and known. To go beyond the familiar requires a conceptual leap into areas of risk and uncertainty. Yet such leaps are essential to accomplishing the large-scale changes needed in today's environment. Thus designers should plan to depart from the status quo as much as possible when designing. This departure will offset the natural tendency to stay with the known and to treat the current organization as a constraint rather than a target of change.

Conclusion

The second stage of self-design involves designing or redesigning the organization for higher performance. It is essentially a creative process of creating something new out of existing ideas, information, and ingenuity. Designing starts with identifying the criteria against which alternative designs will be judged. The activities included in laying the foundation for self-design provide the input for identifying design criteria. The next step involves generating alternative designs. The designs may be concerned with fine-tuning the existing organization, imitating the innovations of other organizations, or creating an entirely new organization from scratch.

8

Guidelines for Designing

Whether designers attempt to fine-tune the status quo, imitate others' innovations, or design from scratch, they must generate new organizational features and processes. These designs can vary from relatively simple changes in methods of working to comprehensive changes in several design components, such as structure, work design, information and decision systems, and human resource practices. The following general guidelines can facilitate the creative process of generating new designs.

Minimize Constraints

All organizational designers face real constraints that are unchangeable in the short term—laws cannot be broken, capital investments cannot exceed the organization's ability to provide funds, and so forth. In addition, however, organizations have sacred cows that are deeply embedded in the way members think about what is possible. These kinds of constraints may be more imagined than real. For example, the following kinds of statements often include untested assumptions: "That's the way we've always done it, and it's always been one of our strengths." "We've found through experience that our methods work quite well." "People can't work effectively if they have two bosses."

When assumptions are untested, they can unduly constrain the designs that are considered. Designers are far more likely to develop innovative designs if they start with few untested constraints and modify new designs as real constraints are discovered than if they begin the design process with a host of implicit assumptions. They can seek to minimize constraints by assuming that they do not exist unless there is unequivocal evidence to the contrary. This practice may seem risky in light of the suspicion that much design rework may be required when designers discover that something really is a constraint. However, it may be more effective to modify a new design to meet newly discovered constraints than to leave things the way they were previously because of imagined constraints.

The designers from Hi-Value's Human Resources department (Chapter 7) were redesigning their unit to provide more customized, business-related services to the several diverse businesses they served. As previously designed, specialized expertise was housed in powerful corporate groups that developed and enforced corporatewide solutions to human resource issues, including corporate compensation systems, selection and recruiting, and performance appraisal. Most designs that were proposed to create more business-specific responsiveness entailed assigning specialized expertise to particular businesses and allowing diversity in these practices.

Several members of the design team were continually shackling the design process by pointing out the staffing and skills limitations in the department. As novel designs were suggested, these members warned that the unit did not have sufficient employees with appropriate skills to staff the new designs. This practice blocked the creative process and led to fewer design options. To break through this impass, designers were encouraged to set aside concerns about staffing limitations temporarily and to create an ideal design to provide customized services. Later the team modified the design to account for staffing constraints. They decided to resolve these problems through skills training, redeployment of personnel, and staged implementation of the new design. Had the designers not created the ideal organizational design before dealing with the staffing constraint, they would probably have ended up with minor modifications of the status quo instead of the substantial redesign that they achieved.

Generate Multiple Designs

Designers frequently have problems creating designs different from the status quo. They may experience difficulty in breaking through existing assumptions or in envisioning new ways to do familiar tasks. Designers can expand their horizons by generating multiple alternatives. This practice should increase the chances of developing novel designs and of finding one that meets the criteria. For example, designers may be able to synthesize an excellent design from a variety of less-promising alternatives.

Design teams can achieve diversity in designing by dividing into subgroups. Each subgroup designs independent of the others and then shares its results with the whole team. Diversity can be enhanced by having similar people in each subgroup yet differences in membership across groups. However, this practice runs the risk of generating unresolvable conflict when each homogeneous subgroup becomes committed to its own favored design. Another option is to form subgroups with different kinds of people in each group. This practice localizes conflict within the subgroups and enables multiple perspectives to be taken into account in generating each group's design. This latter approach may reduce diversity, but it enhances the likelihood that a design that is acceptable to all stakeholders will be generated.

After subgroups have generated multiple designs, the entire design team should discuss them and make choices. This practice may include identifying the concepts underlying each alternative and examining their similarities and differences. The team can then choose a concept they want to build on and fill in the details with parts from the different options. Alternatively the team may simply choose a design from among the options or create a hybrid design out of several of the proposals.

The design team from Hi-Value's Human Resources department broke into three subgroups to generate alternative designs. Each subgroup was composed of people with a diversity of experiences and perspectives. The three groups created a total of five structural designs for reorganizing the unit. When the entire team examined these options, they discovered that two organizing concepts underlay them. One concept combined all the department's planning and development functions into a strategically oriented group, and all the business services into an operationally oriented group. The other concept grouped all the units' services, both strategic and operational, according to the kind of employee being serviced—management or nonmanagement. The team assessed these two organizing concepts against the design criteria. After choosing one of them, the team picked specific features from the various structural designs that embodied the concept. During this discussion, they also generated new design elements that were not included in any of the original proposals.

Minimally Specify Designs

In creating organizational designs, designers should specify only those features necessary to communicate the core concepts of the design. They will have to think through the design at a level of detail sufficient to determine whether the values can be embodied in an achievable design. However, within broad design prescriptions, there are likely to be several potential design solutions, and the best solution is likely to vary in different areas of the organization or unit. Consequently the details of the design can be determined during implementation by those whose ownership is required to make it work.

For example, designers in Hi-Value's Human Resources department determined that certain personnel tasks would be decentralized into each business unit of the firm. They worked through several potential approaches to decentralization to satisfy themselves that it could be accomplished in a manner that truly served business needs. However, they left it up to the human resource manager of each unit to work with the managers of the previously centralized personnel functions to determine how many positions would be required, how the tasks would combine into jobs, and what level of skill would be required of employees performing the personnel tasks.

There are at least three key reasons for minimally specifying designs. First, existing knowledge of high-performing designs provides only general prescriptions for change, and designers need to translate that information into structures, processes, and behaviors suited to their situation. This requires considerable trial-and-error learning; members make the designs more detailed as they learn how to make them work. Second, in today's world, organizational designs are likely to have a short half-life as environmental and technological changes make them obsolete. Minimally specified designs have the necessary flexibility so they can be modified if the circumstances demand. Third, minimally specified designs allow implementers to have some freedom in tailoring the design to their needs. This increases understanding of and commitment to the design and thus increases the chances that it will be implemented.

In minimally specifying designs, designers should try to communicate the logic underlying the design. This practice may include the key features of the design and/or the core concepts that were used to generate it. Designers in the Long-Life Pharmaceuticals plant

(Chapter 3) listed the following design features as critical for implementing self-regulating work teams: a group task forming a relatively self-completing whole; members having the skills and information to control the nature of material and information coming into and leaving the group; and members having the skills, information, and freedom to control how the task is accomplished, including work methods and task assignments. The details of how to do these things were left to be worked out by the teams themselves. By working through these issues, team members would come to understand the practical realities of the design features, would have a sense of being able to influence them, and would begin to feel ownership and responsibility for the design.

Iteration

Designing should be considered a series of iterations, where alternative designs are generated, assessed, and modified until a final proposal is chosen. This design cycle helps ensure that the different elements or components of the design fit each other and that the entire design satisfies the criteria. Because the design of an organization constitutes a total system, it is important that the various design components fit together. However, design teams generally consider the components one at a time. To achieve fit among them, the team must keep repeating the iteration process throughout all the components. Each iteration may result in modifications of components to better match each other and the design criteria. Designers may need to go through several iterations to craft a design that is internally congruent and fits the criteria.

Hi-Value's Human Resources team, for example, initially designed an organizational structure satisfying the criterion of being responsive to the needs of particular businesses. However, another design criterion was that the organization should provide meaningful career paths for human resource employees. When the design team began to discuss career paths, they discovered that their proposed structural design worked against this standard. There were no intermediate positions between administrative roles and functional expert roles. Consequently, there was no pipeline for the higher level positions. In addition, only at the very top of the human resource hierarchy did human resource professionals get responsibility for managing people. The design team altered the structural design so it satisfied both criteria, business responsiveness and career opportunities. A number of intern positions were established to allow administrators to become more strategic in orientation. In addition, an exchange program with the line was designed to allow human resource professionals to spend eighteen months as first-line supervisors in preparation for higher level human resource positions. The kind of iterative process that led to these design modifications should occur until the design team is satisfied with the overall integrity of the design and with meeting design criteria.

Conclusion

This chapter presented some general guidelines for facilitating the designing process that apply whether designers are fine-tuning the status quo, imitating others, or starting from scratch. Regardless of the approach, designers should try to:

- Minimize constraints.
- Generate multiple designs.
- Minimally specify designs.
- Iterate.

IV

Implementing and Assessing

9

The Need for the Action-Learning Process

The last stage of self-design involves implementing and assessing the finalized design. At this point, designers are no doubt eager to bring their design ideas to fruition and to assess the results. Having gone through a systematic process of laying the foundation and designing, designers should feel considerable ownership over the design, understanding its underlying logic and relevance to the situation. Because the design is essentially a hypothesis about what kinds of organizational features are likely to result in high performance, designers must learn how to create those conditions and assess whether they are indeed successful.

Implementing and assessing high-performing designs involve *action learning*—a process where organizational members try out new behaviors, processes, and structures; assess them; and make necessary modifications. They learn from their actions what is needed to make the design a part of normal organizational functioning. This ongoing cycle of actions and assessments also enables members to modify the design to fit the situation as well as changing conditions. Because organizations and environments are not static, action learning never really ends but is a continuous process of improving organizational designs as new conditions are encountered and new learning occurs.

This chapter discusses the need to treat implementation as action learning and describes the action-learning cycle. Three levels of action learning are examined as key to implementing high-performing designs. Practical guidelines for carrying out the two key phases of action learning—implementation and assessment—are presented in Chapters 12 and 13.

Implementation as Action Learning

Organizations have traditionally viewed innovations as relatively discrete entities that can readily be adopted or "put into place" (Cummings and Mohrman, 1987). This adoption perspective includes a number of implementation methods intended to provide organizations with control and certainty over the innovation process. These practices involve maximally specifying innovations in advance and programming the steps needed to implement them. Organizational learning is limited to whatever is required to make the innovation operable and is standardized as much as possible.

Although organizations seek the control and certainty inherent in these implementation methods, severe difficulties arise when trying to apply them to the high-performing designs described in this book. As discussed in previous chapters, these designs do not readily lend themselves to traditional implementation methods favoring standardization, specificity, and control. Existing design knowledge offers only general prescriptions for change, and organizations must learn how to translate that information into specific structures, processes, and behaviors suited to this situation. Organizations invariably encounter unanticipated conditions and consequences when implementing innovations, and they need to learn how to adapt designs to emergent or changing circumstances. Introducing significant change into organizations requires high amounts of member commitment and support, and the implementation must involve members in the learning needed to make the designs work. These conditions for creating high-performing designs underscore the need to consider implementation as action learning, a process involving high amounts of experimentation, assessment, and adjustment (Argyris et al., 1985, Cummings and Mohrman, 1987).

Action learning facilitates two conceptually distinct processes: implementing the design and modifying it. The first learning provides organizational members with sufficient knowledge and skills to implement the design successfully. The second provides members with the capability to refine and improve the design and to adapt it to changing conditions. The action learning needed to support the two processes, illustrated in Table 9-1, is described in the following section.

Table 9-1
Implementation as Action Learning

Why	What	Where
To implement the design	Understand the design	Individual experiential learning; Formal training; Feedback
	Skills, knowledge, and behaviors to enact design	Collective design teams; Staff meetings: Implementation teams
To modify and improve the design	Situation contingencies Supporting changes Environmental changes	Collective design teams; Staff meetings; Implementation teams

Learning to Implement the Design

Although organizational members may have good conceptual understanding of the design, they may not fully understand what is required to make it work until they have tried to implement it. This experiential learning derives from taking action to make the design work. The action produces a variety of consequences that can provide further information about the design and what is needed to implement it. For example, it is relatively easy to describe a computerized design system to an engineer, yet only after trying it out will the engineer gain a deeper understanding of how it changes the nature of the job, the information needed to perform it, and the interfaces with others in the organization. Similarly, managers in firms implementing high-performing practices such as self-regulating work groups, employee-involvement teams, and gainsharing often do not realize until after implementation has started that such innovations entail significant alterations in the way they spend their work day.

Organizational members must invariably develop new knowledge, skills, and behaviors in order to implement new designs. Members of self-regulating workgroups, for example, must learn group problem-solving skills, whereas supervisors need to learn how to facilitate group development. Learning these new behaviors is often not a straightforward training process, such as acquiring technical skills. Many of the requisite behaviors gain meaning only within the context of a new set of values and a new way of understanding the organization. Supervisors of self-regulating workgroups, for example, may need to alter their concept of hierarchical control before they can place a priority on developing group self-control. They need to reconceive their role as facilitating the group to get its task accomplished rather than as planning and controlling group task performance.

Much of the action learning aimed at implementing the design occurs individually as members try out new behaviors and rely on feedback from others to determine whether the behavior is congruent with the values underlying the design. Supervisors who continually reject ideas from employee-involvement teams may require feedback from the team, peers, or management to help them see how their actions are contrary to the espoused values of allowing employees to use their judgment to make work improvements. Although such learning involves individual development, it often occurs best in groups consisting of members who are mutually involved in the change program. Members can interact in supportive ways, giving and receiving feedback from each other. They can share ideas and suggestions and mutually reinforce each other's learning.

Action learning in group settings can also facilitate implementation by helping members develop a collective understanding of what is needed to implement the design. Such shared knowledge is particularly important for high-performing designs that tend to rely on coordination among organizational members for implementation. Members must have a sufficiently shared view of the design to coordinate their joint efforts. To help members develop mutual understanding of the design, formal training, which tends to be aimed at individual skill development should be supplemented with opportunities for group learning. For example, an R&D department was simultaneously implementing a computer network and restructuring itself to enhance teamwork among members. In addition to extensive training in the technical use of computers, the unit met regularly to share what they were learning about the computer network and to suggest ways they could use it to enhance their performance. They jointly developed a new way of understanding their own tasks as well as the new design being implemented.

The composition of groups engaged in action learning should reflect the organizational system undergoing change. When new designs call for changes in intact workgroups, learning activities should occur in those settings. This practice can overcome the traditional weakness of individual-based learning where a person's new skills and behaviors may not readily transfer back to the workgroup. Learning in intact workgroups is especially important when new designs alter relationships among members and group norms. Members must jointly learn how to interact and develop norms to support the new design. Similarly, when designs call for increased intergroup cooperation, as for example between union and management, learning in mixed groups can facilitate the development of an effective way for the different parties to interrelate. Members can gain familiarity with each other and jointly learn effective ways to work together.

Organizations tend to underemphasize the action learning required to implement new designs. They often try to implement innovations that require complex behavioral changes through relatively passive methods such as memos, manuals, and formal classroom instruction. These methods work well when innovations are well understood, highly specified, and accepted by organizational members. However, they do not provide the two-way interaction, participant involvement, and rich experience needed to learn the behavioral implications of high-performing designs and to gain commitment to them. Members need to be actively involved in shaping and refining the design concepts and in translating them into concrete structures and behaviors. This involvement requires active methods where members' actions and their consequences are the raw material for learning how to implement new designs.

Learning to Modify and Improve the Design

The second area where action learning can facilitate implementation involves changing and improving the design. This learning is more organizational than individual. It occurs when those responsible for implementing the innovation meet to examine how the change program is progressing and how well the design is working. Learning is directed at detecting implementation errors and correcting them as well as at refining and improving the design. Members may discover that the design needs to be modified to better fit the situation; they may learn new ways to make the design more effective and efficient. Because conditions can change and designs can always be improved, this focus of action learning continues indefinitely, long after the design has been formally implemented. It provides the organization with the built-in capacity to continually push performance barriers and to adapt to change.

Learning to modify the design often results in discovering situational forces impacting its success. These forces generally include technological, environmental, and personal factors that need to be addressed if the design is to fit the situation. Research has identified key situational forces that affect the success of certain high-performing designs, such as job enrichment, self-regulating workgroups, employee-involvement teams, and skill-based pay (Cummings and Molloy, 1977). One such situational force is the growth needs of the workforce; these designs all work best when employees have high growth needs. Designers can learn this knowledge when they lay the foundation for self-design and apply it when they initially design the innovation. They may, however, design an innovation for which there currently is little or no information about situational forces or they may encounter entirely new forces that researchers have not yet identified. If so, designers may inadvertently design an innovation that is inappropriate for the situation.

Through action learning, designers can resolve these problems by closely monitoring the implementation process to discover situational forces and their effects. Based on this information, they can learn to modify the design to better fit the situation. A consumer products firm pioneering in the application of self-regulating work groups discovered that the groups were ineffective in settings where employees had low growth and development needs. Such workers preferred routinized jobs and resisted learning the multiple skills necessary for self-regulation. This response made it difficult to make the design work and led to increased absenteeism and turnover as employees experienced stress trying to perform tasks they were not interested in or qualified to perform. In those situations, the firm altered some of the workgroups to a more traditional design that was more satisfactory to the employees with low growth needs. Once this pioneering firm had discovered the impact of employee growth needs on work design, it used this knowledge to help later design teams develop a selection process for employees for teams in new company facilities.

In addition to discovering situational forces and their effects, action learning can help designers identify organizational features that need to be changed to support the design. As discussed in Chapter 4, the different design components of the organization such as structure, human resource systems, and information systems need to be aligned with each other to achieve high performance. Because the components tend to reinforce a particular mode of operating, changing that way of functioning generally requires alterations in most aspects of the organization. Many high-performing designs are aimed at fundamentally transforming the organization and consequently will require changing multiple aspects of the organization to support and reinforce the design. Implementing self-regulating workgroups, for example, often requires supportive changes in selection practices, reward systems, information systems, and leadership practices (Lawler and Mohrman, 1987). Action learning can help designers make these additional changes. It can help them assess how the design is interacting with other features of the organization, so they can discover what components need to be modified to support it.

A final area where action learning can facilitate modifying designs concerns today's rapid pace of change. As implementation proceeds, changes in the wider organization or environment may render the design inappropriate. This concern is particularly relevant to designs that tend to be complex and take long time periods to implement. Designers are likely to encounter changing conditions before the design can be fully implemented. Action learning can help them identify such contextual changes and modify the design accordingly. For example, after three years of hard work, a large paper mill was well underway implementing mini-business teams and gainsharing. A corporate decision to move to the next generation of paper-making technology rendered significant parts of the design obsolete. Those people responsible for implementing the design learned about the parameters and demands of the new technology and used that information to alter the design to fit them.

Conclusion

A great deal of personal and organizational learning must occur in order to implement high-performing designs and to modify and improve them. Implementing new designs is an evolving process of action learning involving an iterative cycle of actions, assessments, and adjustments. Organizational members start from general design prescriptions and try to enact specific structures, processes, and behaviors believed to be necessary for implementing the design. They subsequently learn how well those changes are progressing and make necessary modifications in both the design and the implementation process. This action-learning cycle continues until members have learned enough to implement the design effectively. The dynamic quality of the process is underscored by the fact that designs can always be improved and conditions can change. Consequently, action learning continues long after the design has been formally implemented and provides members with the knowledge and skills needed to modify and continually improve the organization over time.

10

The Action-Learning Cycle

Action learning enables organizational members to learn from their actions how to implement and improve high-performing designs. It involves an iterative series of actions, assessments, and adjustments intended to provide members with a clearer understanding of the behavioral and organizational implications of the design, and a greater capacity to modify and improve it over time. As shown in Figure 10-1, the action-learning cycle includes four major activities:

1. Taking action to implement and/or modify the design.
2. Collecting pertinent information.
3. Diagnosing progress.
4. Planning to modify the design and/or implementation process.

Organizational members continue to cycle through these activities as they learn how to implement and improve designs. Although the activities are described sequentially in the following sections, they interact and overlap considerably in practice.

Taking Action to Implement and/or Modify the Design

This first set of activities involves actions that are intended to implement or modify the design. These actions include trying out new behaviors, structures, and processes necessary to make the design operable. Members start from broad prescriptions of design features and develop more specific and situation-relevant actions as the learning cycle evolves. Imaginative Systems (Chapter 6) was redesigning to promote greater collaboration between functional departments in shortening the design-to-production cycle for its products. A key design variable was the establishment of interfunc-

Figure 10-1
The Action-Learning Cycle

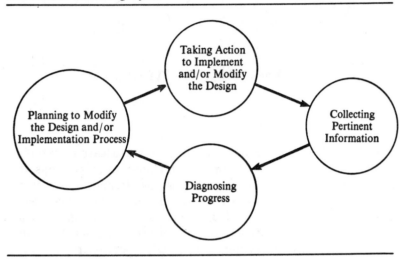

tional teams that worked together from idea generation to shipping. The teams were established as an "overlay" to the regular organization. In time, and after a number of learning cycles, the behavioral consequences of interfunctional teams were fleshed out. The organization learned the teams' optimal composition, how to move people in and out of them at appropriate times, what kind of decision-making authority the teams needed, and how they should relate to the functional authority structure of the organization.

Collecting Pertinent Information

This second set of learning activities involves collecting data on how the design is working and how the implementation process is progressing. It provides members with information that members can use to diagnose the progress of the implementation process and the success of the design. Data are collected periodically, usually at three- to six-month intervals, and fed back to members to help them gain a clearer understanding of the behaviors needed to enact the design and to help them plan the next steps for implementing and modifying it.

Three kinds of information are typically collected in self-design:

1. Features of the design itself.
2. Design outcomes.
3. Contextual aspects of the organization and its environment.

(Chapter 12 deals in greater depth with the data collection process.)

Design Features   The first type of data concerns the different features of the design being implemented. As discussed in Chapter 5, designers specify valued organizational conditions they are trying to create through self-design and design features that need to be implemented to attain them. There is a growing body of knowledge identifying these design elements, and designers can learn that information when laying the foundation and designing. In cases where existing knowledge does not apply to the desired design, designers can derive specific design features by closely examining the valued organizational conditions. During implementation, designers need to gather information on design features in order to assess how well the design is being implemented. Such information can help them identify which design features are progressing adequately and which ones need special attention and additional implementation action.

Information about design features typically includes participants' perceptions of how well the design is being implemented as well as company records of design implementation. As discussed in Chapter 6, perceptual data can be gathered in a variety of ways, ranging from informal interviews with selected members to standardized questionnaires given to all participants in the implementation process. We have spent considerable time helping organizations develop instruments to measure key dimensions of high-performing innovations, including job enrichment, self-regulating workgroups, employee-involvement groups, skill-based pay, goal setting, gainsharing, and participative management systems. Great care is taken to ensure that the instruments provide valid and reliable measures of the design features. Moreover, questionnaires are supplemented with selected interviews and company records whenever possible.

Design Outcomes The second type of data involves the valued performance and human outcomes designers are trying to achieve. These data include specific performance measures such as product quality, productivity, and costs, as well as human measures such as absenteeism, organizational commitment, and work satisfaction. Some of these measures are collected routinely in organizations for purposes of accounting and control. They can provide a longitudinal measure of whether the design features are having intended effects. Some of the human outcomes such as satisfaction and commitment require perceptual data that can be collected through periodic interviews and questionnaires. Organizations may require assistance from consultants skilled in survey design and measurement issues to develop tailored instruments for measuring participants' perceptions of performance and human outcomes. Standard instruments are also readily available (Taylor and Bowers, 1972; Seashore et al., 1983; Van de Ven and Ferry, 1980). Some commercial instruments, such as those offered by International Survey Research and Opinion Research Corporation, also provide normative or comparative data.

Organizational Context This third type of data includes situational forces that can affect the success of new designs, including technological, environmental, and personal dimensions. Information about these contextual factors can help designers either tailor or adjust the design to fit the situation. As suggested in Chapter 6, designers initially collect data on these forces when diagnosing the situation. They use this information to design high-performing designs suited to the situation. During implementation, designers should continue to gather contextual information to assess whether the situation is changing in a way that would make the design inappropriate. If so, they can alter the design accordingly. In one electronics company, individual-based job designs became ineffective when the introduction of computerized design and manufacturing systems made tasks more interdependent. The changing conditions called for more group-based work designs where members could coordinate their actions around interrelated tasks. In Imaginative Systems (Chapter 6), the trust required for successful operation of the interfunctional new product teams eroded when business conditions led to layoffs. The firm adapted to this change by providing companywide communication of business information and by establishing a task force to determine how to maintain the interfunctional cooperation even though people were protecting their own turf and feeling stressed by having to do the work with fewer people.

Diagnosing Progress

This third stage of the action-learning cycle involves analyzing the data collected earlier to discover whether the implementation process is progressing as intended and whether modifications are necessary. As suggested in the first section of this chapter, members can learn from the consequences of their actions what behaviors are necessary to implement the design as well as how to modify and improve it. The success of these diagnostic activities depends largely on how well members can engage in problem-solving. They need to examine information about design features, outcomes, and context in order to detect implementation problems and to diagnose their underlying causes. This examination provides the understanding necessary for planning how to modify the design and implementation process.

Because much of this diagnostic activity is conducted in groups, typically in intact work teams or implementation committees, members need to be proficient at group problem-solving. This proficiency may require rudimentary training in problem-solving and group dynamics, usually beginning when laying the foundation for self-design. It may also require ongoing process consultation when the group is actually diagnosing implementation progress. Members must learn how to work together to identify problems and discover their causes. They must learn how to examine and improve group process so that members solicit and listen to divergent interpretations of the data, reconcile differences, weigh contributions appropriately, and arrive at a sufficient consensus of the problem and its causes to plan jointly for improvements.

Planning to Modify the Design and/or Implementation Process

This last set of learning activities involves planning to change the design or implementation process based on the preceding diagnosis. Designers may have discovered that certain features of the design are not being implemented effectively, that new behaviors are not being enacted correctly, or that changes in the context are rendering the design obsolete. Based on these diagnoses, designers need to make specific plans to alter or adjust the design and the change program to achieve the desired results. This alteration may include myriad minor adjustments aimed at making the design operable. A glassmaking company trying to implement skill-based pay had to alter the skill blocks, training program, and performance appraisal process in order to make the design acceptable to employees. In some cases, the design may have to undergo significant change in order to achieve success. Long-Life Pharmaceuticals (Chapter 3) had to alter drastically its self-regulating group design when it discovered that the technology was more certain and less interdependent than expected. The company changed to a more individual-based, routine work design. This change also required fundamental changes in selection and training practices in order to attract people who would desire such jobs.

Case Study: The Colorful Paint Company

A concrete description of the action-learning cycle involves job enrichment in a paint-making plant of the Colorful Paint Company. As part of a companywide effort to enhance employee involvement, the plant's design team, comprising a cross-section of managers and employees, decided to enrich a number of routine jobs on the shop floor. Preliminary diagnosis revealed that many employees were dissatisfied with their traditional jobs, and that ample opportunities to enrich them existed. The design team learned from the available literature that job enrichment included at least three key design features: task discretion, task variety, and feedback of results. These features can improve employee motivation, satisfaction, and productivity, particularly for people having high growth needs (Hackman and Oldham, 1980).

The design team began to translate these general prescriptions into specific actions and procedures. They began the implementation process by trying to make the following organizational changes:

- Supervisors were encouraged to provide employees with more freedom over work methods and task scheduling (task discretion).

- Tasks were enlarged to include certain inspection activities (task variety).

- Specific information about task performance was given directly to employees (feedback of results).

Prior to implementation, the design team used a standard questionnaire to gather baseline data on employees' perceptions of the design features, expected outcomes, and growth needs. Company records also provided time-series trend information on each employee's level of production.

About six months into the implementation process, the design team collected information on how job enrichment was progressing. Data from the questionnaire and company records showed that the expected outcomes—motivation, satisfaction, and productivity—were essentially unchanged from the period prior to implementation. Employee perceptions of discretion and feedback also showed negligible change, whereas perceptions of task variety improved significantly from the baseline time period. Although employee growth needs were relatively high, examination of the distribution of scores revealed a few people with low needs for growth at work.

Diagnosis by the design team identified a number of implementation problems and their probable causes. Two of the design features were not being implemented as intended—employee discretion and feedback of results. This problem explained in part why the expected outcomes failed to occur. Informal interviews with supervisors and employees revealed that simply encouraging supervisors to give employees more freedom over work methods and schedules did not really work. Many supervisors were unclear on how to change their traditional leadership styles to more participative methods. Some clung doggedly to their autocratic styles, whereas others went overboard with what some described as a "country-club" approach. In terms of feedback of results, interviews revealed that many employees could not understand the data in its current form and consequently ignored it.

Diagnosis also revealed that for those few employees with low growth needs, job enrichment was inappropriate. They preferred more routine forms of work and felt dissatisfied with having to make task decisions and to inspect their own work. For them, job enrichment was demotivating.

Based on the diagnosis, the design team planned a number of modifications of the implementation process. It decided to institute a leadership training program for supervisors. The program would be aimed at providing the knowledge and skills needed to adapt leadership styles to a more participative context. It also decided to have staff from the information-systems department meet with selected employees and jointly design a feedback process that would be understandable and useful to workers. Finally, the design team specified a small number of jobs that would remain routine and assigned them to any employees wanting to leave enriched jobs.

The design team continued with the implementation process over the next several months. Then, about eight months after the previous data collection, another round of information was gathered using the questionnaires and company records. This time the data showed that expected outcomes improved moderately over the baseline period. Both measures of task variety and feedback of results were significantly higher than the baseline period and were rated rather high by employees. However, perceptions of employee discretion over work methods and schedules remained low and relatively unchanged from the baseline period.

Continued diagnosis of implementation problems revealed that the leadership training program was seen as useful conceptually, but it did not translate into changed supervisor behaviors on the shop floor. Discussions with corporate human resource specialists helped to explain the problems of transferring classroom training to work situations. Selected interviews with supervisors also suggested the need for on-line coaching and counseling during daily work hours. Diagnosis also revealed that supervisors' pay and performance appraisal had little connection to participative behaviors. There was little external incentive to behave participatively.

Based on this diagnosis, the design team planned two key modifications of the implementation process. First, it decided to ask human resource specialists to work closely with supervisors to provide them with feedback and coaching as they performed their daily tasks. This intense interaction would occur once or twice a week for a four-month period and would focus on behavioral changes in supervisors. Second, with the support and sanction of top management, the design team created a task force comprised of managers and reward-system specialists to assess current supervisory reward practices and to propose changes for more tightly linking participative behaviors to rewards. It was hoped that these proposals could be implemented within the next six months.

This action-learning cycle continued for about nine more months until further data showed the design team that job enrichment had been implemented effectively and achieved expected results. Then, data collection and diagnosis continued at about one-year intervals to help supervisors and employees modify the design to fit changing conditions and continually to improve it.

At first glance, it might appear that the Colorful Paint Company simply misdiagnosed its situation and implemented a faulty design. What we referred to as "learning" might as easily be seen as rectifying their errors of diagnosis and design. However, it is important to understand that there is a great deal of uncertainty involved in the self-design of high-performing organizations. Implementation is risky, as it involves trying out practices that have never been used in this context. It often requires a "leap of faith" that the innovative design features will work. Often, organizations may lack the knowledge or the courage to implement a particular feature, or they may misinterpret their diagnostic data and implement design features that solve the wrong problem. Political factors may cause an organization to start with a "baby-step" toward the preferred design, hoping to create a critical mass of supporters for further action.

In sum, any and all of these factors may be present and may interfere with a design team's ability to design perfectly and implement on the first try. None of these factors constitutes evidence that self-design has failed. Rather, it is because of the inevitability of these factors that the iterative action-learning cycle is needed.

Conclusion

Action learning is a cyclic process of taking action to modify the design, collecting information and diagnosing progress, and modifying the design or the implementation process. Information is collected about the design features, outcomes, and the organizational context. Through this learning cycle, the design team may learn that additional implementation activities are needed, additional design features are required to create organizational congruence, or that further design activities are needed due to changes in the environment.

11

Levels of Action Learning

Learning must occur at three fundamental levels if organizational members are to gain the capability to self-design high-performing innovations: single-loop learning, double-loop learning, and deutero learning (Bateson, 1972; Argyris and Schon, 1984).

Single-Loop Learning

This lowest level of action learning involves detecting and correcting differences between the organization's current and desired states. It occurs within an existing frame of values and is aimed at discovering deviations from those values and taking steps to correct them. The action learning in the Colorful Paint plant (Chapter 10) primarily involved single-loop learning. The design team had a relatively clear idea of the valued outcomes and conditions it was trying to promote through self-design. It collected data to assess how well implementation activities were satisfying those values and conditions and took specific steps to correct implementation errors.

The major outcome of single-loop learning is behavioral change. Participants learn the kinds of behaviors that are needed to correct the situation and achieve valued results. At Colorful Paint, the supervisors learned new skills for conducting meetings, the information-systems staff learned how to design more meaningful feedback systems, and workers learned how to inspect the results of their work and make decisions about work methods and scheduling. All of these behavioral changes were intended to correct implementation errors and to promote certain valued outcomes and conditions.

Single-loop learning works best when designers have a clear idea of desired values and conditions, can readily detect and diagnose deviations from them, and can generate appropriate remedies. These conditions generally exist when members are fine-tuning their organization in order to modify and improve it. They accept the values underlying the current design and aim their learning activities at better actualizing them.

Single-loop learning can encounter problems, however, when designers are trying to transform the status quo by significantly altering valued outcomes and conditions, such as might occur when imitating others' innovations or zero-based designing. In these situations, designers may have trouble detecting and diagnosing deviations between the desired and actual design. Designers may have only vague ideas of what the organization should look like to achieve valued outcomes. Moreover, the new values may only be partially understood and adhered to during the early stages of implementation.

At Colorful Paint, increasing employee discretion turned out to be difficult to achieve. In part, this problem resulted because the supervisors did not have participative skills and did not know what behaviors to adopt to transfer decision making to workers. Behavioral skills training alone did not solve the problem because supervisors were unable to enact those behaviors in an actual work setting. Single-loop learning was inadequate because the values that supervisors held and that were reinforced by organizational reward systems worked against the desired behaviors. Furthermore, supervisors were unable to recognize when their own behavior violated the espoused values of the change effort. Consequently, new values were needed and systems had to be designed to support the new values before significant behavioral change could occur. Single-loop learning was not adequate.

In change situations that require value shifts, there will be ambiguity about whether particular design features are being implemented correctly and whether certain values are being actualized. In these situations, single-loop learning needs to be supplemented with a higher level of inquiry aimed at changing values, called double-loop learning.

Double-Loop Learning

This second level of action learning is concerned with changing existing organizational values. It typically arises when designers encounter value conflicts during implementation. Although new values may have been set when laying the foundation for self-design, underlying conflicts between those values and existing organizational norms and procedures may not have emerged yet, but they need to be resolved before designers try to implement innovations promoting the new values. For example, in trying to implement participative management practices that promote values of employee decision making and involvement, designers may discover that providing employees with more task discretion runs counter to prevailing norms promoting managerial control. Those existing norms may block implementation of participative management; they may offer strong resistance to enhancing employee discretion. The norms lead to behavior that presents a paradox for employees. They have been "ordered" to take initiative and responsibility in a tightly controlled context.

To resolve this conflict, designers must first recognize that it cannot be corrected within the frame of existing organizational values—an exercise in single-loop learning. Rather, they must undertake double-loop inquiry that results in changing the values themselves. Specifically they must develop a behavioral understanding that organizations do not have to be controlled by controlling people. Rather, organizations can be controlled by empowering people to perform their jobs well. Our experience suggests that cognitively grasping this concept is easy; behaviorally, learning it is quite difficult.

Double-loop learning involves both individual and group change. Some have argued that such inquiry involves a time-consuming process of individual change that must precede organizational change (Argyris and Schon, 1978). Others have proposed that changing values is essentially a social process that must occur at the group or organizational levels (Cummings et al., 1985). Our experience with double-loop learning suggests that both views are partially correct. A great deal of personal change must occur in order to depart from traditional values and models of organizing. This change generally involves trying to understand personally the values implicit in the new design and embarking on experiential learning that involves feedback on how one's behaviors fit with those values. Colorful Paint began to make progress in changing supervisory behavior when it provided coaches to give immediate behavioral feedback to supervisors about their behavior, the impact it had on subordinates, and the values and assumptions that were exhibited.

For many people, the experiential learning that comes from being part of a design team and trying to enact new values and behaviors can provide a foundation for double-loop learning. Stronger evidence that the learning has occurred requires that the changed behavior generalize to other on-the-job situations as well.

At the group or organizational levels, double-loop learning derives from collectively trying to change the organization. Group norms that promote gathering diverse and often discordant information and sharing divergent views can help design teams develop a collective understanding of the status quo, the valued future, and how to reduce the distance between them. By more fully understanding where they are trying to go and the barriers they are encountering, design teams can commit more fully to the new values and can enrich their implementation efforts. This group learning vividly unfolds when diverse stakeholders are jointly implementing a change. Union/management design teams, for example, generally go through a series of learning cycles in which each party points out to the other areas where their implementation behavior violates agreed-to values. In this way, various stakeholders can learn to trust one another sufficiently to open themselves up to understanding the multiple perspectives and to enrich their own appreciation of events and relationships. Through this process, members learn to attach different meanings to their own behavior.

In some cases, double-loop learning leads designers to return to the valuing stage of self-design in order to reassess the new values and possibly modify them. Designers may initially set unrealistic values, mainly because they have not fully explored their behavioral implications or tried to enact them. As designers gain experience trying to implement valued changes, they may discover through double-loop learning that the costs of promoting certain values outweigh the benefits. Rather than abandon the values altogether, designers may change them to more achievable levels.

An example of such redefinition of values occurred in a chemical plant that initially set extremely high values for employee involvement. It wanted to develop self-managing teams and multi-stakeholder decision making about all issues where the workforce had a stake. Several months of trying to change managerial behaviors to enhance employee discretion resulted in only moderate improvements in employee involvement. After considerable diagnosis and self-assessment, the team reluctantly agreed that the initial values were unrealistic in the context. There was a considerable amount of environmental change that required frequent changes in product, process, and cost structure. Managers could not concentrate on or believe in the appropriateness of transferring discretion and involvement when they had to introduce sometimes unpopular changes quickly and efficiently. They were continually initiating change and making survival-oriented decisions that violated employee expectations for team autonomy. Because of the uproar this created, they vividly learned the incongruity of unilateral top-down change, even when environmentally required, with the expectations of self-managing teams to be partners in decision making and to control their own functioning.

Consequently, they revised the values (jointly) to more modest levels and refocused their efforts to achieve them. The new focus was to empower employees to have an impact on their future job security by providing training in quality and process control. This change enabled teams to be technically more self-sufficient and to influence directly plant performance. They found that as the teams became technically more self-sufficient, the original values of self-management became more possible to achieve. The revised expectations provided a more realistic foundation for employee involvement and reduced members' frustrations and skepticism with the change process.

Deutero Learning

This highest level of action learning is perhaps the most important for designing high-performing organizations. It is aimed at improving the previous two levels of inquiry, or more simply, learning how to learn. When engaged in deutero learning, designers examine factors in their own situation that facilitate and inhibit single- and double-loop learning. They then try to create more effective learning processes in the organization. Because implementing high-performing innovations typically requires several iterations of the action-learning cycle, designers should have ample opportunities to assess their learning processes so they can improve them. Deutero learning should be explicitly built into the implementation process.

An example of deutero learning occurred in the Newtel steering committee when it was implementing a continuous improvement process that relied on the creation and empowerment of self-contained work areas. Although structural changes were made, improvement in operational measures were not forthcoming. The steering committee and other design teams in the company continually attributed this situation to being on the "learning curve."

They looked for and found signs that things were improving. After many months, they became discouraged and examined their own processes. They discovered that their behavior discouraged learning. These same patterns of behavior characterized the company as a whole and were part of the reason why the continual improvement process was not achieving success. Specifically they always focused on positive indicators and explained away the negative data with phrases such as "we're working on it," "it's improving," and "we're aware that it's a problem but we've got someone looking at it." In addition, they challenged the credibility of those who brought negative data to their attention and took consolation in the "fact" that the messengers of bad news were unaware of the actions underway to take care of the problem. Only after they started treating negative information seriously, dealing with the problems and setting deadlines for improving the functioning of the work areas, did performance begin to improve. They had to learn how to learn.

Implementing high-performing designs places heavy demands on organizational learning processes. In large organizations, several hierarchical levels may be simultaneously engaged in self-design. Formal committees may be created for managing the designing and implementing activities. Deutero learning can help organizational members integrate these different bases of learning and ensure that the different participants have the requisite skills and information to enact the design and modify and improve it. This policy is particularly important when organizational members who have not been part of the design team are responsible for implementing the design. They must be afforded opportunities to learn about the design and to learn from their implementation activities how to enact and improve it.

Identifying the Appropriate Learning Level

Design teams may find themselves operating at any or all three levels of learning: single-loop, double-loop, and deutero. Unless the organizational members are skilled in the action-learning process and organizational norms support it, most design teams will spend a significant amount of time in deutero learning—learning how to learn. The self-design process is an action-learning process and cannot be effectively enacted by groups that do not learn to learn. Throughout the self-design process, design teams have a dual focus:

1. They will be going through the stages of self-design.
2. They will be focusing on their own learning process to detect norms and behaviors that are interfering with self-design.

Teams that are redesigning within an existing value framework must become good at the problem-solving process that is the essence of single-loop learning. Organizations striving for increased efficiency and improved processes may primarily use single-loop learning procedures. Within most self-design efforts there are a number of such design challenges. The desired conditions are clear (for example, reduced waste, utilization of fewer resources, and higher quality output).

The challenges of today's environment demand redesign that alters existing values and the establishment of new conditions that are difficult to picture from within existing frames of reference. High-involvement management is one change that requires double-loop learning. Another is the transition to "total quality" that is being espoused by many companies and that often includes the concept that quality is meeting customer requirements. This is a new value for organizations that have traditionally assumed that their own engineers can define quality. An organization that attains this value will have a whole new set of organizational features that establish a different relationship with customers and that have not been well tested to date. Organizations have had to strike out on their own and "invent" new ways of working with customers. The internalization of this value and the embodiment of it in new design features requires double-loop learning: overcoming traditional assumptions and trying out new features that embody new assumptions.

When double-loop learning is required, design teams have to set up internal learning processes that enable them to reframe, that is, to challenge their own assumptions and begin to see their world differently. Design teams can often detect the need for double-loop learning when they become aware that they are trying to sustain two conflicting values in the same design (for example, tight hierarchical control and employee initiative). Another signal that double-loop learning is required is when organizational members plead that they "do not understand" concepts (such as customer responsiveness) that imply changed authority relations or objectives and are resistant to establishing the design features that embody them. This often signifies that the design team has undergone double-loop learning, but the remainder of the organization has not. Reframing experiences that enable others in the organization to go through double-loop learning will have to be part of the implementation plan.

Conclusion

Action learning occurs at three levels. Single-loop learning includes detecting and correcting deviations between the existing and preferred organizational design. Double-loop learning involves changing the values underlying the design itself and is required when new designs require different action logics or values. Deutero learning concerns learning how to learn and is often required to detect behavior patterns that prevent learning from experience.

12

Guidelines for
Implementing the Design

We have described the process of implementing and assessing high-performing designs as action learning, involving an iterative cycle of actions, assessments, and adjustments. Because this is a highly uncertain and emerging process, designers will need to figure out for themselves how best to carry out the learning activities for their particular situation. We can offer some general guidelines, however, based on our experience with self-design. We have learned that successful self-design efforts share certain organizational conditions that facilitate implementation of new designs.

This chapter presents these guidelines. It is important to emphasize that they are not intended as imperatives for self-design success. Rather, they might even be viewed as outcomes of the kind of learning that design teams go through as they implement new designs. In most cases, the organizational conditions will not be present when self-design starts, and through time designers will learn how to develop them as they implement new designs. Indeed, self-design enables the kind of learning that is necessary to create these facilitating conditions.

Take an Active Leadership Role

Leaders must take an active role in all phases of self-design, especially the implementation stage. Although self-design is a highly participative process, line managers have responsibility for managing it and seeing that relevant stakeholders are included. They should help organizational members recognize the need for change, create a vision of the desired future, and ensure that the changes are implemented and become part of the organization's normal functioning (Beckhard, 1988; Tushman et al., 1988; Tichy and Devanna, 1986).

In self-design, line managers generally share these leadership functions with members of the design team. This is a relatively straightforward process when self-design is carried out within existing work units. Here, members of the design team consist of the formal leader and members of the unit, and leadership for self-design follows the normal chain of command. In cases where self-design has been delegated to a design team that sets broad design guidelines for the rest of the organization, line managers need to legitimize those efforts. They must be involved sufficiently with the design activities to become committed to them and to provide the leadership necessary for implementation.

Active senior leadership is particularly important during the implementation phase. Senior managers need to confer authority upon the change efforts and show active support for them. Because employees look to higher level management to determine the importance of the changes, executives must be visibly involved in the implementation process if it is to be taken seriously. They need to model the desired new behaviors and promote the new designs that are being created. They need to show publicly that new behaviors are expected and will be rewarded.

Senior executives in Newtel (Chapter 2) showed their active support for the teamwork needed to make the company more competitive. They were the first to examine and improve the teamwork of their own team. They received training complementary to that received by lower level employees. The senior executives appeared regularly in training classes to state expectations and to answer questions. They demonstrated commitment to self-design by being open to feedback, soliciting input about implementation progress, and responding with constructive support. This active leadership occurred regularly and helped to sustain momentum for change.

Grow Champions

Implementing high-performing designs requires a sustained commitment of resources and support. This commitment is likely to occur when there is a sufficiently broad constituency of participants to champion the change effort. Typically the early phases of self-design will have created a group of champions, but the list must grow considerably during implementation so that all implementing units and stakeholders continue to support the design efforts.

The primary method for growing champions is to encourage selected participants to become increasingly involved in the change process. They must be given the opportunity to contribute to the decisions, to achieve visibility, and to influence the design and implementation process in ways that help them achieve their goals. Membership and especially leadership in various design teams, task forces, and coordinating committees can create such champions. Placement on these groups should be strategic, to develop ownership and competency in self-design among those who are currently influential as well as among those who are expected to move into powerful positions in the future.

For example, one firm that pioneered the development of high-involvement concepts in the United States started its efforts by identifying a group of unionists and managers who were expected to rise to influential positions over the next few years. The company placed these "young turks" on key committees and task forces involved in designing the initial high-involvement efforts. This procedure provided a ready stock of champions for subsequent corporate changes, particularly as the initial participants gained power in their respective union and company organizations.

Manage the Transition Process

Implementing organizational designs involves moving from the existing design to the desired new one. This movement involves a transition period during which members are learning to implement the new design (Beckhard and Harris, 1987). Because the organization may have to operate in the transition mode for some time, special arrangements should be made for managing the transition period. In large-scale change efforts, this transition may require appointing a special project manager who can coordinate the different implementation activities. This person should have considerable social, political, and integrative skills to perform effectively. At Newtel (Chapter 2), the project manager of the implementation process was a highly regarded line manager who many believed to be on a fast track to the top of the firm. He helped to coordinate the diverse implementation activities and to design special mechanisms for goal-setting, accounting, and rewarding during the transition period.

It is important to emphasize the dynamic and iterative nature of the transition process, where feedback assesses actions that affect subsequent actions and so on, until members learn enough to implement the design. Moreover, members' vision of the desired design will likely change and develop over time as members learn more about it and envision possibilities that they could not have previously imagined.

Figure 12-1 illustrates the evolving nature of the transition process. As implementation proceeds and organizational learning occurs, members gain the capacity to modify both the design and the implementation process. This modification leads to a series of continuously refined designs. An aerospace firm, for example, began self-design with the intention of setting up a quality circles program to encourage ideas and improvements from the bottom of the company. During implementation, designers discovered that the circles often spent their time on issues that were not central to the performance of the firm. They subsequently modified the program by supplementing the circles with task forces whose efforts were aimed at high payoff concerns. A further iteration of action learning

Figure 12-1
Transition Process

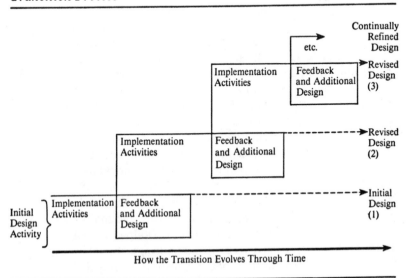

How the Transition Evolves Through Time

resulted in another revised design: the development of intact work teams having key performance information and the ability to manage themselves with accountability for costs, schedule, and quality.

Don't Neglect the Political and Cultural Aspects of Change

Implementing organizational change involves simultaneously attending to three aspects of the change process: technical, political, and cultural (Tichy, 1983). The technical part includes the content of the desired design, such as structure, work design, and information systems. The political aspect involves who controls decision making and how rewards are allocated, whereas the cultural part concerns the values and norms shared by members. The three aspects of change are intertwined so that changes in one part generally require corresponding modifications in the others.

During implementation, self-designers tend to focus on the technical aspects of change, often neglecting the political and cultural parts. They may have trouble mustering the power needed to implement the design and establishing the cultural norms to support it. Consequently, the implementation process must be designed to address explicitly the political and cultural parts of change in addition to the technical aspects. This procedure may include expanding the change process to include a wider set of stakeholders, particularly those who have not been directly involved in the designing activities yet whose understanding and support are needed to implement the design. It may also involve going beyond the technical changes being implemented to include plans for changing the distribution of power and rewards in the organization and the kinds of behaviors that are considered legitimate. At Newtel (Chapter 2), for example, the companywide design teams focused on the strategic business changes, whereas local implementation teams tended to fixate on alterations in the authority and reward structures that would be required to implement them.

Integrate Implementation and Learning Activities

Action learning is integral to implementing high-performing designs. It enables designers to learn what is required to implement the design and refine the implementation process itself. Consequently, learning must be explicitly built into the implementation activities. Designers must create specific methods for collecting data about the progress of the design and implementation process; they must design methods for analyzing the information and devising appropriate modifications. Alternatives for designing this action-learning cycle are discussed in Chapter 13. Here, it is important to emphasize that all units involved in implementing the design must be engaged regularly in this learning process. Moreover, when several units are involved in the change process, leaders must develop a nonthreatening way to make the learning from the different units public so that it becomes part of the collective wisdom of the organization. Several organizations that we have worked with have instituted yearly learning conferences where representatives from units throughout the company share their self-design experiences. In particular, these organizations developed conference norms that support joint learning and recorded their experiences in the form of general principles that can be disseminated in the organization.

Communicate Openly

Because self-designers typically modify the design as they learn, implementation is ambiguous and cannot be defined fully in advance. A key challenge is to cope with the natural skepticism of organizational members who have a low tolerance for ambiguity. They need to be kept informed about the implementation activities, particularly when they are not directly involved in designing them. Unfortunately open communication about implementation goes against the instincts of many managers who feel the need to appear "in control" during the transition to a new way of operating. This reaction frequently leads to an overly rigid implementation process where employees feel intentionally uninformed.

Although the participative nature of self-design will naturally help to reduce ambiguity about implementation, additional forms of communication may be necessary, including periodic meetings, written reports, and informal discussions. In implementing strategic changes at Model Simulation Systems (Chapter 4), the company held periodic communication meetings in all operating units undergoing change. At the meetings, a current progress report was given, and members of the companywide design team solicited input about how the implementation process was progressing and how it could be improved. This information exchange enabled members to hear a consistent story about the implementation and to support changes and share ideas about how to improve it.

In large-scale change efforts where representative design teams have been designing on behalf of others, communication informs other key stakeholders about the need for change and the substance and rationale behind the new design. A well-designed orientation process can show management support for the changes and provide employees with an opportunity to raise concerns and make suggestions. At Newtel (Chapter 2), the companywide design teams created an orientation program to communicate to the rest of the firm the new design and implementation process. The program had four communicative purposes:

1. To share information about the new design.
2. To provide opportunities to input into the implementation process.
3. To demonstrate the commitment of management and union leadership to the changes.
4. To collect information about what implementation problems to expect.

Once the designing phase was complete, the design teams developed a two-hour orientation for all 20,000 employees of the company. The orientation occurred in natural task groups, and it was conducted by the supervisor of the unit, the department head, and an appropriate union officer. This procedure ensured that no group heard about the new design until their leaders were sufficiently informed and committed to conduct an orientation. As the leaders carried out the orientation, they shared some of the skeptical comments and concerns that were being heard throughout the organization and admitted that they themselves had some concerns about the viability of the new design, given many of the long-held norms and practices existing in the firm. This openness helped employees raise their own difficulties with the design. This feedback was further facilitated by the leaders who asked employees what they thought would have to change in order for employee involvement to work in their unit. Members of the corporate design teams later held meetings with the leaders who had conducted the orientations in order to discuss the concerns that had surfaced, to solicit ideas for improving the implementation process, and to encourage the leaders to take an active stance in removing the barriers to change.

Motivate Change

Successful implementation depends on both the quality of the design and the motivation to make it work. Laying the foundation for self-design provides members with the knowledge and skills to develop a high-quality design. Motivation to implement, on the other hand, depends on members' beliefs that their implementation efforts will be effective and will result in valued outcomes (Campbell et al., 1970). These beliefs can be troublesome during implementation as members may be unsure of how to perform effectively or whether certain performances will be rewarded. Moreover, members may be cynical about organizational change. They may have a "program mentality." As programs come and go in the organization, employees develop a sense that personal investment in change is often unrewarded and that they can outlast any new program just by laying low and letting it burn itself out.

Figure 12-2 illustrates the elements affecting people's motivation to implement a new design. It shows that personal motivations to change depend on expectations about both personal and organizational change efforts and their consequences. Employees need to believe that their own efforts to implement the design and to change behavior will be successful and will lead to valued outcomes. They must have similar expectations about organizational efforts at change.

Self-designers must create an implementation process that facilitates these expectations about change and its consequences. They need to provide members with the skills and information they need to implement the design and to perform effectively. They must ensure that those performances are directly tied to outcomes that members value. Organizationally, designers need to show that key stakeholders support the design and are willing to change accordingly. Resources for change need to be available along with a clear plan to manage the transition process. The technical efficacy of the design needs to be communicated as well as its likely performance outcomes and, of course, any early successes.

Figure 12-2
The Motivation to Implement

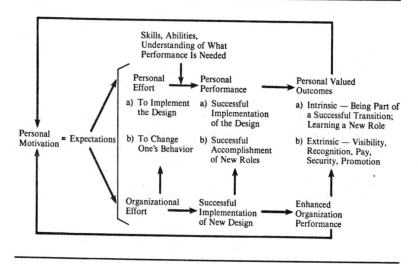

Encourage Local Input and Accountability

In large-scale change, design teams typically generate minimal specification designs that other units can further refine and implement. These units are responsible for local design and implementation, and encouraging their input enhances the ownership of the design and its suitability to the situation. It runs the risk, however, that local design teams will deviate significantly from the valued direction of the overall organization. Thus higher level design teams must maintain responsibility for both coordinating the local change efforts and ensuring that progress is made. Local implementing teams should be made accountable to the higher level teams for ensuring that the changes conform to the broad values and guidelines of the overall design.

This accountability can take several forms. When design teams are an integral part of the managerial hierarchy, the formal leader of each team can hold members accountable for implementing the new design through the establishment of goals and the appraisal process. In the Colorful Paint factory (Chapter 10) when it was implementing high-involvement concepts, the plant manager jointly set goals for implementing the new methods with his staff. He subsequently reviewed each member's progress toward those objectives and linked a major part of the annual pay increase to individual and team goal achievement. Each staff member carried out a similar goal-setting and appraisal process with his or her direct reports.

When design teams are parallel to the managerial hierarchy, such as an ad hoc team composed of a cross-section of organizational members, explicit steps must be taken to ensure that the full weight and authority of the formal leadership are behind their efforts. This goal can be accomplished through a formal mandate from top management outlining guidelines and support for the design team's efforts. Such sanction needs to be supplemented with a reporting system that enables the design team to assess regularly how implementation is going and to identify units that are progressing too slowly or in the wrong direction. Ad hoc design teams cannot simply issue a design directive and expect the rest of the organization to follow. They must actively manage the implementation process, including surfacing information, providing assistance, and influencing the direction of change.

Design teams should use the authority of the formal hierarchy as much as possible to implement new designs. They must create review and feedback systems that constantly direct organizational members' attention to how well the implementation process is going. The organization's appraisal, feedback, and reward systems are key tools in establishing accountability. A major part of members' performance appraisal should be their role and contribution in implementing the new design. Staffing and reward practices must also take this factor into account. Implementing new designs can receive a real boost when those who are doing a good job of implementation receive recognition and rewards and are put into positions of increased responsibility. Some organizations engaged in self-design use each staffing decision to make a public statement about the importance to one's career of learning to operate the new design.

Train Flexibly to Reinforce the Design

Training is an important tool in implementing new designs. Although we have discussed the need for training when laying the foundation for self-design, it is important to reiterate two key points when implementing the design. First, training should be as flexible as possible so that it can be used differently depending on the needs of units implementing new designs. One way to achieve flexibility is to break the training program into modules, enabling its various components to be mixed and matched to the situation. Moreover, as implementation proceeds, new training needs will likely surface, and the inadequacies of current approaches will likely be discovered. Flexibility of training can help implementers modify the training program accordingly. Like the new design itself, the training needed to support it will undergo continual refinement and improvement.

A second key issue related to training for implementation concerns the settings where it occurs. Whenever possible, training should occur in settings that reinforce the design. For example, if intact work teams are undergoing change, training should occur in those groups. Members can readily apply the training to their situation and can use it to reinforce necessary behavioral changes. In the new-plant start up at Long-Life Pharmaceuticals, all managers, supervisors, and union leaders were initially trained together. This configuration reinforced the kind of cooperation and coordination needed to bring the plant on line. Once employees were hired, part of their general skills training occurred in the total group. This training underscored the need to cooperate, which produced economies of scale in training skills applicable to all members. The remaining part of the training having to do with specialized skills took place in members' respective functional teams.

Promote Self-Design as an Ongoing Priority in the Organization

It should be clear by now that self-design is successful to the extent it becomes an ongoing priority in the organization. Design and implementation activities can be expected to ebb and flow with the circumstances. When a new design is being implemented, self-design is likely to involve considerable time and resources. At other times, it will involve fine-tuning and refining what is already there, and it will seem like a normal way of everyday operation.

To achieve priority in the organization, self-design must receive committed resources so that members gain the skills, information, and sufficient time to create high-performing innovations. Design activity should not be limited to a small design committee or project management team, but it must be diffused throughout the organization so that workgroups can learn how to design and improve their own situations. Thus, managers must learn how to manage an action-learning process as well as the tinkering and tailoring necessary to improve their units and adjust to changing conditions. Perhaps most important, corporate leaders need to instill values and processes that facilitate learning from doing. They need to reinforce learning from mistakes and failures, rather than trying to stomp them out through persecution and control.

Conclusion

This chapter presented a number of organizational conditions that designers can learn to create to facilitate implementation of high-performing designs. Self-design enables the kind of learning necessary to create the following conditions for implementing new designs:

- Take an active leadership role.
- Grow champions.
- Manage the transition process.
- Don't neglect the political and cultural aspects of change.
- Integrate implementation and learning activities.
- Communicate openly.
- Motivate change.
- Encourage local input and accountability.
- Train flexibly to reinforce the design.
- Promote self-design as an ongoing priority in the organization.

13

Guidelines for Assessing the Design

Assessment is an integral part of the action-learning cycle that enables designers to implement and improve high-performing designs. It includes collecting pertinent data about the design and its outcomes and using that information to diagnose whether the design is being implemented effectively and whether it is achieving valued outcomes. Such learning helps designers plan for necessary changes in their own behaviors, the implementation process, and the design itself.

This chapter presents practical guidelines for carrying out the assessment part of action learning. Attention is directed at making assessment a highly relevant and useful feedback process for designers, and an integral part of their ongoing learning. This method contrasts with more traditional approaches that tend to view organizational assessment as a discrete event carried out after implementation, with heavy emphasis on objectivity and methodological rigor.

The guidelines are aimed at minimizing many of the negative dynamics typically associated with evaluation. For many people, assessment is threatening. It raises fears of inadequacy and incompetence. It can point out errors and raise the possibility of more work. It can negatively impact members' career progress. Moreover, members are frequently suspicious of organizational assessment because it is based on concepts and techniques that are unfamiliar to them. Consequently, the guidelines in this chapter are aimed at making assessment minimally threatening and maximally useful to organizational members.

Throughout this chapter, examples will be given from the assessment that was conducted at Long-Life Pharmaceuticals

(Chapter 3). This plant was a greenfield start-up, designed to use optimal manufacturing systems and to have high employee involvement through such design features as extensive information sharing and training, quality improvement procedures, a flat structure, self-managing work teams, and skill-based pay. Its assessment process was one of the most complete we have seen, and it allowed several major design modifications and improvements while, at the same time, allowing Long-Life Pharmaceuticals to ascertain the overall effectiveness of the design.

Take Frequent Assessments During Implementation

Especially during the early stages of implementation, members need to progress rapidly through the action-learning cycle. They need to know quickly and repeatedly whether the different features of the design are being implemented correctly and whether they are having the intended impact on valued outcomes (Cummings and Mohrman, 1987). This information helps members detect errors in the implementation process and helps them learn how to enact the behaviors required to make the design operable.

A quick and inexpensive way to collect data about implementation is a short, informal interview with selected members. In the early stages of helping members start up the Long-Life plant, we conducted such interviews at monthly intervals during the first few months of implementation. The interviews lasted about twenty minutes each and took place over the course of a work day. At the end of the day, we summarized the interview data and fed it back to the design team responsible for managing the implementation process. (Table 13-1 provides a sample interview for periodic, quick feedback on implementation.)

In large-scale change efforts, designers should supplement the interviews with more extensive surveys about members' experiences with the changes and with more quantitative measures of performance. These data may be collected and examined as often as every six to nine months during the transition period. They provide a good baseline for assessing progress and enable designers to discern trends that may signal problems or successes.

At Long-Life, the informal interviews were supplemented with organizational surveys administered to all members of the plant every six months during the two-year start-up period. The surveys

Table 13-1

Sample Interview Format for Frequent, Quick Implementation Feedback

1. How is the implementation of the (new design) going?
   What aspects are working well?
   What aspects are not going so well?
2. Has there been sufficient orientation?
   Do the people in your work area have good information about the changes that are being introduced?
   Do they see the need for change?
3. Is the training adequate for implementation?
   If not, what additional training is needed?
4. Are there barriers to change? What are they?
5. Is there support for the change?
   From the people you work with?
   From your managers?
   From top management?
   From support and staff groups?
6. Do you have concerns about the changes that are being introduced?
   Do you think they will help the organization perform better?
   What suggestions do you have?

covered the major features of the design as well as members' perceptions of valued outcomes. These data were summarized in bar graphs and fed back to intact work teams for purposes of diagnosis and subsequent modification of the local designs. Each team used its own data to learn new behaviors and make necessary adjustments. Trends in weekly records of absenteeism and team productivity also guided this learning process.

The plantwide design team at Long-Life examined aggregate survey and performance data to detect more global needs for modifying the design and implementation process. Negative trends in turnover of production workers and unsatisfactory productivity and quality gains signaled the design team to do additional diagnosis and to revisit its values. It discovered that the production process was less interdependent than originally assessed and that the team-based work design should be modified to a more individually oriented one. The plant was able to keep most of the other design features, such as a flat structure, quality-improvement activities, and information sharing.

Assess the Design's Overall Effectiveness Periodically

Once organizations have gone through the action learning required to implement the new design, they should step back periodically and evaluate its overall effectiveness. This evaluation tells designers whether they should drastically alter the design, discard it altogether and recycle through the earlier stages of self-design, or continue to support and refine the design. Such periodic assessment needs to occur every twelve to eighteen months and should be continued indefinitely so members have a built-in mechanism to monitor the design and seek ways to improve it. Long-Life Pharmaceuticals employed a companywide survey process every eighteen months to evaluate the plant's overall design and performance. The plant management team and each of the operating and staff units used this information to assess whether the design needed to be changed significantly. More informal assessments of how to improve performance were built into the daily work routine of the plant.

High-performing designs are not easily evaluated in a rigorous, scientific way. Outcome measures can be affected by a variety of factors independent of the design, including the economy, turnover of key personnel, new technology, and so on. Although designers cannot readily control for these alternative explanations, they should use the following three guides to enhance the validity of their assessment efforts (Seashore et al., 1983):

1. *Longitudinal measurement.* Measures of design features and outcomes should be taken repeatedly over relatively long time periods. This method permits analysis of trends in the data so that designers can ascertain whether the design and outcomes are moving in the valued direction. Ideally the data collection should start before the design is implemented.

2. *Comparison unit.* It is desirable to compare results of the design with those of other units, plants, or companies

having different designs. Although it is impossible to get a comparison group identical to the new design unit, most organizations include a number of similar work units that can be used for comparison purposes.

3. *Statistical analysis.* Statistical methods can be used to rule out the possibility that results are caused by random error or change. A variety of statistical techniques are available for assessing the results of high-performing designs, and designers can apply those methods or seek help from those who can (Cook and Campbell, 1976).

After three years, Long-Life was able to evaluate the overall design in a convincing manner. Its performance data showed sharply upward trends after the initial eighteen-month start-up and after work design changes were made early in the second year. At twenty-five months, performance surpassed that of all other Long-Life plants producing similar products. The new plant was continuing to improve in stark comparison with the relatively flat performance levels of the other plants. A corporatewide attitude survey revealed that the new plant was statistically more positive on most dimensions and among all employee groups than its sister plants, despite the stresses of continual growth and the need to accommodate new and untrained supervisors and employees. The evaluation data were so convincing that the corporate operations group planned to introduce self-design to its other manufacturing plants.

Figure 13-1 illustrates a complete assessment process extending from the initial, frequent assessments of the implementation period through periodic evaluation of the overall design after it has been implemented.

Use Diverse Data-Collection Methods

Designers should use a variety of methods to collect data for learning about the design, including interviews, observations, questionnaires, and company records. Each method has certain strengths and weaknesses, and designers should combine several different methods to gain a comprehensive and relatively valid picture of how the implementation process is progressing and whether valued outcomes are being promoted.

Company performance measures are typically the most "objective," but by themselves they provide few clues to the factors

Figure 13-1
Assessment Activities

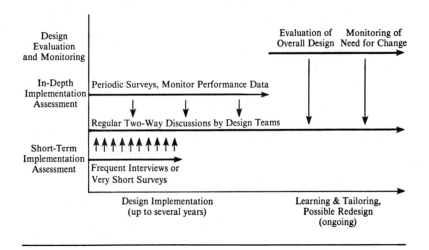

contributing to changes in performance levels. Survey questionnaires are an efficient method for gathering perceptual data on a
variety of issues from a large number of people. Because there is little
interaction with the respondents, however, it is impossible to delve
more deeply into their responses and to uncover specific needs and
concerns not included in the survey. Interviews provide more in-
depth discussion and identification of issues than surveys. They can
allow designers to gain a rich description of how members are
experiencing the implementation process and the new design. They
are limited to relatively small samples, however, making it difficult
to know how representative the data are. Group discussions, such as
staff meetings or focus groups composed of selected members, enable
a number of people to share and discuss their views and to arrive at
a consensus about the implementation process and the new design.
Drawbacks of these groups are the time demands and the risk that
poor group process will thwart information sharing.

Long-Life Pharmaceuticals used a typical combination of
data-gathering methods for assessing high-performing designs. It
starts with relatively simple interviews with selected members about
how the implementation process is progressing. These interviews

provide quick feedback and may uncover issues that need to be probed further, perhaps in a survey to a larger number of participants. A survey is then administered to provide systematic perceptions of many of the design features and members' reactions to them as well as attitudinal data about employee commitment, satisfaction, and involvement. The survey data and company records that provide trends in performance, absenteeism, and the like are fed back to various discussion groups, such as intact work units and design teams. Group members delve into the meaning of the data and arrive at a sufficient consensus about problems and their causes to take corrective action.

Use Information to Learn, Not to Punish

Designers can become "trapped" into defending the new design regardless of its success because their careers and rewards are linked to its effectiveness (Campbell, 1969). They then stick close to the status quo rather than risk trying an innovative design with uncertain results. They seek positive findings that affirm their design choices rather than discordant information that suggests the need to modify them. Eschewing valid information and honest assessment, trapped designers fail to carry out the organizational learning required to implement and improve the design.

To reduce the chances that designers will become trapped, corporate leaders can assess and reward them both for performance and for how well they carry out the learning process. For example, those who quickly discover mistakes and problems and make necessary adjustments should be rewarded. Leaders must also allow designers a certain period of time for learning how to make the design work without being unduly punished for their performance shortcomings. During implementation, performance may actually decline as employees learn how to make the design work. Once the design is operating normally, however, designers can be assessed on more typical, performance-based measures.

At Long-Life, managers of the new plant were concerned that their modification of the work design would be interpreted by corporate leaders as a failure to make the team design work. Fortunately corporate management had stayed close enough to the design efforts to understand that some aspects of the design might not fit the situation and that significant learning and modification were necessary to make the design a high-performing one. Consequently, corporate leaders were able to see the new plant as a learning opportunity for the rest of the company. They based a large part of the annual bonuses of the plant managers on how well they carried out the learning process.

Involve People in Interpreting Their Own Data

Data used for assessing designs are inherently ambiguous. They do not literally speak for themselves but require considerable interpretation in order to detect and analyze causes of implementation and design problems. Self-design should involve all relevant organizational members in interpreting and analyzing their own data. This procedure provides deeper meaning to the information and enables members to share different views and arrive at understanding and ownership of the data.

Data collected from intact work teams should be fed back to members of those units. Team members can jointly analyze the information and draw conclusions for modifying and improving their unit. When a special design team is responsible for the implementation process, members of intact work teams can help that team assess the data they have provided. At Long-Life, work teams received their own survey data, and the plantwide design team received aggregate data for all units. Representatives from each work team met with the design team to discuss their issues and proposed modifications, thus facilitating learning among units with different experiences and successes.

Include Skeptics in the Assessment Process

As discussed earlier, assessment data are always ambiguous and open to multiple interpretations. Indicators can be selected to favor particular views, and people can focus on data that support their beliefs and desired outcomes. These biases can severely limit the information used for implementation and can lead to erroneous conclusions about modifying and improving the new design. Thus multiple perspectives should be considered in assessing high-performing designs. Among the multiple stakeholders having interest in self-design, there will always be those who are skeptical about the relevance and effectiveness of the new design. Rather than exclude such skeptics from the assessment process, their views need to be considered. Skeptics can serve as "devil's advocates," raising questions and providing interpretations of data that might otherwise be ignored or overlooked. They can challenge the premises of designers and uncover problems that are critical to design success.

Including skeptics, particularly influential ones, in the assessment process has the added advantage of directing their attention to the self-design process. They can become an integral part of the problem-solving process, rather than an external irritant. This participation increases the chances that skeptics will become committed to self-design. Unless their views are represented in the assessment process, it is unlikely that they will become committed regardless of the data. Such involvement also shows skeptics that the new design is not sacred, but can be modified, changed, or discarded altogether. It shows them that self-design is a process for discovering ways to achieve high performance, not a particular design solution.

Diffuse Learning Broadly

In situations where the total organization or a major subpart is undergoing redesign, learning from self-design should be diffused broadly throughout the organization. This differentiation provides members who may not have been directly involved in the designing activities with information about the new design and the rationale underlying it. It also keeps them informed about what modifications are being made during implementation and how these alterations fit with valued outcomes.

Diffusing such learning broadly throughout the organization helps to ensure that learning from self-design does not become encapsulated, confined mainly to the design teams or committees responsible for the overall change project. At Long-Life, newly formed design teams spent time talking with more experienced teams to hear about what pitfalls to avoid, key success strategies, what to expect in implementation, and the stages that the experienced teams had gone through.

Broad diffusion of self-design learning also helps to clarify the changes occurring in the organization and to show that they are not random but part of an overall learning process. During an intensive implementation process, a good strategy is to set aside a portion of each staff and work-unit meeting to discuss the implementation effort—what is being learned and what changes are being made. At Long-Life, all teams were aware that there might be a change in the work design, and they knew the data pointing to the need for such a change. Consequently, they were not surprised by, and in fact had had considerable input into, the eventual change to an individual work design. This procedure contrasts with organizations that have "announced" three or four major reorganizations over a several year period. Each announcement is typically preceded by rumors, and organizational members can only surmise that top management has changed its mind again. Members experience the organization as a ship out of control that keeps changing direction and layering change upon change.

Developing a reliable communication system to share plans, learning, and accomplishments throughout the organization is one of the biggest challenges of self-design. Such a system enables members to orient themselves to what is happening during a time when changes may seem arbitrary and turbulent. It allows for two-way communication so that members can question what is happening and feel heard by those in charge of the change program.

Conclusion

This chapter presented a number of practical guidelines for assessing high-performing designs. The following suggestions were meant to make assessment minimally threatening and maximally useful to designers:

- Take frequent assessments during implementation.
- Assess the design's overall effectiveness periodically.
- Use diverse data-collection methods.
- Use information to learn, not to punish.
- Involve people in interpreting their own data.
- Include skeptics in the assessment process.
- Diffuse learning broadly.

V

Organizing for Self-Design

14

Structures, Norms, and Resources for Self-Design

Now that we have described the self-design strategy, there are a number of organizing issues for carrying it out effectively. These strategies have to do with structuring the self-design process, creating norms to promote necessary kinds of design behaviors, and allocating resources to the process. We will discuss organizing issues in this chapter and address special applications of self-design to large-scale change efforts in Chapter 15.

Structuring for Self-Design

Once they have decided to proceed with self-design, organizations need to determine who should be initially involved in the process. This choice depends largely on the complexity of the organization or unit to which self-design is being applied.

The self-design strategy can be used by organizations or subunits of varying complexity. In the simplest case, a small work unit may use it to design itself to perform a certain task. Perhaps new equipment is being introduced, and a new task design is needed. In this situation, the structure for self-design is relatively straightforward. The members of the unit, including the supervisor and employees, are the primary stakeholders who must learn how to make the new design work and must be committed to implementing it. They are directly involved in all stages of self-design, from laying the foundation and designing to implementing and assessing the new design.

At a higher level of complexity, such as a manufacturing plant or a department within an organization, self-design is typically structured to follow the managerial hierarchy. The design process starts at the top level and cascades downward throughout all organizational levels and units. Units at each level design themselves within the broad values and parameters set by higher level units. This procedure ensures consistency of direction, while allowing for local variations and modifications. For example, we have worked with several greenfield manufacturing sites where self-design starts with the plant manager and his or her direct reports, plus representatives of key stakeholder groups such as unions. They manage the overall self-design process, typically generating a mission and value statement for the plant, and designing the broad parameters of its structure, operating systems, information systems, and human resource practices. Each member of the plant manager's team is responsible for moving the design process down into her or his own unit, where similar yet more circumscribed design activities occur, and so on down to the lowest level operating units. Generally there is considerable negotiation and feedback across the different plant levels as participants test boundaries, experiment with design modifications, and learn new things. Through time, units at each level within the plant gain the capacity to self-design.

The most complex level of self-design occurs when a total organization or large division needs to transform itself, for example, an electronics firm that seeks technical compatibility between products produced by autonomous divisions using different technical specifications. Here self-design is likely to have a complex structure with specially created design teams managing the design process for the entire organization. For example, design teams composed of selected representatives of the autonomous divisions might focus on different aspects of the compatibility problem. A higher level steering committee might coordinate the outcomes of the different design teams. We will describe alternative ways to structure such large-scale design tasks more fully in Chapter 15.

It is important to emphasize here, however, that self-design is equally relevant regardless of the complexity of the situation. It is applicable whether the design task is comprehensive and involves all aspects of the organization, or focuses on a major component, such as the organization's human resource practices or information-processing systems. Self-design is relevant to new organizations such as greenfield sites or entrepreneurial firms and to mature organizations transitioning to a new design. How the organization structures itself for self-design will vary, of course, in all these situations.

Norms to Support Self-Design

Because self-design generally occurs in design teams, either natural work units or specially created groups, team norms can affect how well members jointly perform the various learning, problem-solving, and designing tasks. In Chapter 1, we described the emerging norms of high-performing organizations in today's environment, and developing those norms during the design process is the first step in creating an organization that embodies them. Specifically, the following norms are supportive of the kinds of behaviors needed for self-design:

- Open sharing of information.
- Tolerance of mistakes.
- Value of information and expertise over hierarchy.
- Valuing differences.
- Teamwork.
- Flexibility.
- Valuing involvement and adaptation to the situation.

Unfortunately, these norms are foreign to many traditional organizations. Furthermore, when people feel threatened or insecure, as they often do when facing turbulent environments and the beginning of organization change, they often behave in the opposite direction of these norms. In such situations, people often become more closed, rely on hierarchy, and protect their individual security sometimes at the expense of the organization.

Consequently, it is critical that design teams learn how to develop those norms during the self-design process. Developing the norms is an integral part of self-design and occurs throughout the change process. Team members should explicitly set appropriate norms, continually assess how well the team is behaving with respect to the norms, and make necessary adjustments in their behaviors. Members must pay as much attention to the social processes underlying self-design as they do to the content issues. A process consultant can facilitate this norm development. External consultants may have the edge in the early stages of self-design since they are unlikely to be afraid to challenge existing organizational norms and do not share the organizational fears that members do. It is important to emphasize, however, that members should develop the skills to address and resolve their own process problems. Thus, as self-design unfolds, members gain a greater capacity to develop and behave according to the norms described earlier.

Resources for Self-Design

Organizing for self-design requires a commitment of resources through time. The exact amount and content of those resources can vary enormously depending on the complexity of the design process. Designing a small unit, for example, may take only a small amount of time and budget, whereas a more complex project can involve considerable resources, such as extra leaders for design teams, a project manager, heavy time investments, and a budget. At least four types of resources should be considered when getting started with self-design: leadership, expertise, dedicated time, and budget.

Leadership

Leaders of design teams should be acknowledged organizational leaders who are respected and have the ability to excite and involve others. They may come from the existing managerial ranks or be recruited from other roles such as union leadership, staff specialists, and informal leaders. They will play a leadership role internal to the design team, helping members learn to carry out self-design. Perhaps more important, however, is their role in the larger organization, mustering support and resources for self-design. Key people may have to be freed up and placed in these leadership positions. They will require the training and support necessary to manage the self-design process.

Expertise

Most design teams deal with organization features that are quite technical and require special expertise to design, such as the design of jobs, information systems, organization structure, and human resource practices. When the expertise exists within the organization, staff experts should be assigned to design teams or serve as resources to them. When design teams push beyond the experience and expertise of internal resources, they should employ external consultants who have requisite experience and skills. Consultants also frequently have a great deal of experience with change processes and can provide useful information in planning the self-design activities. When the design process is extensive, the organization should consider hiring or developing self-design experts internally. By choosing high-potential individuals to develop expertise in this area, the organization can build its own internal cadre of self-design specialists to help members manage change and improvement through time.

Dedicated Time

Although not absolutely essential, self-design proceeds more smoothly and quickly if it is performed by a core of people who can spend considerable time on the change effort. Ideally the design team is dedicated full time at least during the stages of laying the foundation and designing. Even during implementation and assessment, a good portion of designers' time should be available so they can serve as the focal point for the action-learning process. In addition, it may be useful to include experts at appropriate times during the design process. For example, an automotive systems design company that was implementing mini-business teams assigned a human resource specialist, an information-systems expert, and a communication specialist full time to the change effort during the implementation period.

Budget

Although it is difficult to specify in advance how much self-design will cost, it is advisable to create an estimated budget. This budget forces design teams to think about and make a reasonable estimate of resources so that the organization is not caught by surprise by costs exceeding what it can or will spend. Budgeting forces managers to examine their real commitment to this kind of change effort.

A key cost that is often neglected is the time that it will take for people to attend meetings, go through training, attend orientations, fill out surveys, answer interviews, and so forth. It is often assumed that line managers can absorb these costs. This premise stems from lack of familiarity with how many "extraordinary" costs are incurred in changing an organization. To reduce the likelihood that managers will be placed in a situation of conflicting expectations, they should be allowed to budget for these extra costs rather than being caught in a reward structure where the costs of self-design harm their self-interests.

Conclusion

This chapter discussed how to organize for self-design. Once self-design is chosen as a change strategy, members must decide how to structure initially the process around specific design teams. Then, they must begin to develop appropriate norms for those teams and provide necessary resources, including leadership, expertise, dedicated time, and a budget.

15

Applications for Large-Scale Change

Self-design is increasingly being used in large-scale change situations, involving a total organization or large division and addressing multiple design components. Although we have referred to large-scale applications throughout the book, our experience suggests that designers can lose sight of the overall structure for self-design in such complex change efforts. Consequently, this chapter provides an overview and summary of the total design process with special attention to the structures and roles that may need to be created to manage large-scale change.

Structuring for Large-Scale Change

Multiple Design Teams

How many and what kinds of design teams depend on the design task at hand; how large and diverse the organization or unit is that is being designed; how complex the design task is; and how much diversity will be tolerated in the design that is being implemented in different organizational units. Multiple design teams may exist at different levels in the organization—the corporate, the division, and the department levels. Similarly, multiple teams might address different features of the organization—information systems, work designs, and human resource practices.

Cascading Design Teams. An organization can use a single design team to design a small work unit. Members of the unit would comprise the design team, and it would include the diversity of perspectives within the unit and would address most of the contingencies and design requirements that are likely to be faced.

Multiple design teams at different organizational levels will be required to design a larger organization or unit, such as a total corporation or a division. Such large-scale design efforts face two key design tasks. The first task is the *macro* design that affects all units. It includes corporate values, the design of large structural units such as divisions and departments, and design features that are to be common to all units to ensure cultural uniformity, to enable economies of scale, or to promote coordination between interdependent units. The second task is the *micro* design of each subunit. This task includes local modifications of the macro design as well as supplemental designing of such local features as workflow, job design, and operating procedures. Figure 15-1 illustrates the notion of cascading design teams at different levels of the organization.

The primary arrow in Figure 15-1 goes downward, illustrating that each level in the design process develops values, parameters, design features, and guidelines that serve as a context for, and consequently constrain, groups at embedded levels in the organization. This directionality reflects the need for overall strategic direction to be set by a group with organizationwide responsibility and for that group to ensure that all organizational units are moving in compatible directions. Note that this higher level team may include representatives from various hierarchical levels of the organization.

From the perspective of the higher level team, lower level teams are implementation teams whose function is to devise ways to implement the values, parameters, guidelines, and design features that the higher level team has generated. To implement these broad directions, however, lower level teams will be required to design new features, clarify values, make the desired behaviors more concrete, and tailor design features to fit local requirements. At each level, the design is more fully defined, and the design team is working with fewer degrees of freedom.

In Figure 15-1, there is also an upward arrow at each level, indicating that embedded levels should have the opportunity to influence the broad design decisions that are made, to provide feedback about how well they function within the area that is their purview, and to generate innovative approaches that may be diffused throughout the organization. This upward arrow is thus important both to the designing process and to the action learning cycle.

Newtel created a design structure similar to the one displayed in Figure 15-1. At the top was a corporate steering committee that

Figure 15-1
Cascading Design Teams

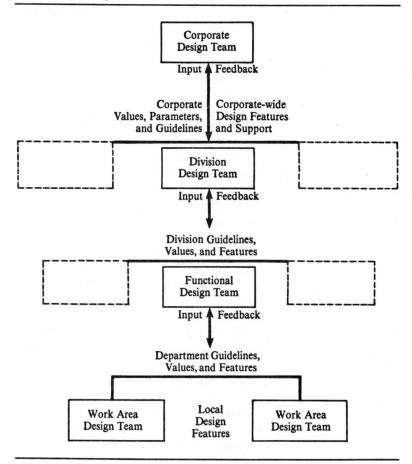

provided a broad strategic direction and design requirements that included responsiveness to market forces and emphasis on teamwork and quality improvement. Within these broad guidelines, divisional design teams started the actual organizational design work. Because various divisions performed different tasks and were structured quite differently, the corporate steering committee provided only broad organizational guidelines. It established a multistakeholder "council" to provide ongoing coordination of change efforts, to review operating and human outcomes, and to identify needs from a multi-stakeholder perspective. The corporate design team also developed training programs to provide a common language and set of skills to describe and enact the new thrusts for market responsiveness, employee involvement, and quality improvement. They also defined a wide variety of teams that could be set up to get employees involved, monitor interfunctional market issues, and address quality problems.

Divisional councils (which served as design teams during the transition) determined how to apply the training and which of the various teamwork approaches fit their structure and technology. In some cases, they also initiated innovative structural changes. In each department within a division, a small cross-sectional group was charged with addressing the "nitty-gritty" design and implementation issues, such as how to schedule time for change activities and how to communicate information.

Some organizations make the mistake of designing all the details of a new design at the highest level and then trying to "roll it out" through a massive education and implementation plan. Organizational designs that affect all levels of complex organizations are frequently designed by corporate-level design teams that include a diagonal slice of the organization. It is often assumed that the diverse membership of the team will ensure that the new design will be accepted and implemented uniformly throughout the organization. A large, multidivisional manufacturing firm, for example, had a diagonal-slice design team generate a new system for performance appraisal, goal-setting, and rewards. Assuming that the innovations would be well received because the design team membership represented the organization as well, the company planned a six-month, uniform implementation program. The hue and cry that occurred during that period were only slightly less unsettling than the quiet nonconformance that followed. The human resource department that had been charged with implementation spent the next year processing all the negative feedback and redesigning a performance system that met all constituencies' objections but was so average that it met no one's specific needs.

This experience can be contrasted with another firm that used a corporate-level design team to design only the broad parameters of a performance system and established divisional design teams to tailor the specifics of the system to fit their own situations. This multilevel design process enabled broad uniformity, yet engaged each division in a design process that addressed local needs and concerns and promoted local feelings of ownership. It started a learning process that involved people in many parts of the organization in learning a better approach to managing performance, rather than relying on a corporate design team to learn for the whole company. Each division planned its own implementation process, assessed its progress, and made the needed modifications. In some divisions, various functional departments had their own design teams that made minor alterations and oversaw the action-learning process in their respective units. Based on feedback from the divisions, the corporate design team assessed the overall efficacy of the broad parameters of the performance system and also served as a vehicle for the divisions to learn from one another. Within one year, each division was well on its way to implementing new performance-management practices. There was some diversity between approaches in the various divisions, but the broad parameters established at the corporate level remained constant.

Multicomponent Design Teams. The kinds of fundamental design changes that are being demanded of many organizations today often require far-reaching change in many features of the organization simultaneously. Changing from being technically driven to market responsive, for example, requires a new organizational structure that more closely links the technical functions, such as production and engineering, with the market-oriented functions, such as sales and business development. It requires new human resource practices as well as new information systems linking the different functions in the organization. Each design feature will need to be designed by a team having or developing special knowledge of that component, as shown in Figure 15-2. These multiple design teams will have to be aware of each others' efforts and be able to mutually influence one another so that the systems that are designed are congruent with one another. In addition, one design team will have to ensure that these different design efforts are coordinated and fit within a master design strategy. Typically called a *steering committee,* this team will have to gain some knowledge and understanding in each area and determine overall parameters for the change program. More refined development of structure, information systems, and human resource practices can be done by design teams that specialize in each of these components and think them through in depth. These specialized design teams

Figure 15-2
Multiple Component Design Teams

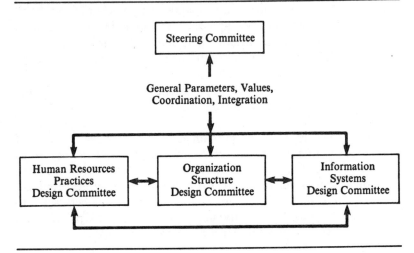

should have some members who are experts in the appropriate content area. The design team responsible for information systems, for example, should include information-systems specialists. However, these specialized teams should also include members from different stakeholder groups, such as user departments, so that their needs are met in the systems that are designed.

The key role of the steering committee in coordinating these multiple-component design efforts should not be underestimated. We have known several companies that were full of specialized teams designing new programs and systems to meet the needs of a changing environment. Each team managed and "owned" its own design effort. It made its own assessment of the needs of the organization in the new environment and assumed that the values that needed to be promoted were those of its discipline—human resources, information systems, or engineering. Because there was little coordination among the design teams, various design efforts resulted in innovations that put conflicting demands on organizational members. One division of a large manufacturing company, for example, had a design committee developing an organizational structure that emphasized teamwork and restructured the entire division into business flexible teams. The committee announced these changes within a week of the completion of a time-consuming effort by corporate staff that updated all job descriptions to fit with the old division structure. To avoid this kind of miscommunication, another firm that we worked with developed a "change board," which was a design team in only the most global sense. It acted as a clearinghouse and coordinating body for all the different change efforts that were going on in the company.

Composition of Design Teams

Design teams at all levels should include the expertise required to generate the design, with the diverse stakeholders having different perspectives and preferences for it. In addition, they must include people with sufficient influence so that the team is perceived as legitimate by others in the organization. Only if all three of these criteria—expertise, multiple perspectives, and power—are met, is it likely that the design team will generate a design that fundamentally transforms the organization while being acceptable to those who must implement it.

The selection of influential and well-regarded members for design teams is critical to the success of self-design. Because self-design generally occurs simultaneously with normal organizational operations, it tends to be perceived as something "extra." Managers often assign members who can easily be freed up for these extra activities. In many cases, individuals who are not being fully utilized or whose organizational roles are viewed as less critical find themselves on design teams. This selection pattern weakens the output of the team because key perspectives are lacking; it reduces the probability that the new design will be implemented because influential organizational members have not been consulted and those on the team have little influence. To guard against this possibility, Newtel created a guideline that all design and implementation teams should include "people who could make it happen and people without whose active interest it would be less likely to succeed." Also, all key stakeholders should be included. These criteria were used each time a design or implementation team was created.

When multiple design teams are in operation, overlapping membership is essential. This overlapping enables the efforts of various design teams to be coordinated from within each team as well as through steering committees or a hierarchy of committees. Because design teams are interdependent—the design of one may constrain or work against the design of another—they are stakeholders of one another and have knowledge that is critical to each other's design efforts. At Newtel, as they were designing a transition to a market-oriented, high-involvement culture, divisional design teams operated within an overall strategy determined by the steering committee. Continual hard feelings resulted when divisional teams were seen as ignoring corporate guidelines or the steering committee was seen as designing with little input from the divisional teams. Frequently, divisional teams would develop a design feature only to find out that the corporate team had been developing an approach to the same issue that was expected to supercede their efforts. Coordination was finally attained by a rotating visitation system whereby one member of each corporate design team attended each divisional design team meeting, and vice versa. In this way, information could be shared in a real-time manner, and misunderstandings and unnecessary effort were avoided.

Linking Design Teams to Existing Organizational Structure

Although design teams are typically given a mandate to design new organizational features, this change alone is insufficient to empower them to make the design a reality. The implementation of the new design will require cooperation, changed behavior, and resources from many stakeholders. Consequently, design teams should consider themselves change agents, and the way they conduct themselves will determine their effectiveness in changing the organization.

Broadly speaking, the change-agent task for a design team is to bring the rest of the organization along as the team progresses in its own development and moves toward the generation of a new design and then to implement a plan. This goal can be accomplished by creating links with the various stakeholders of the organization—those in hierarchical power; various parts of the organization; and different subpopulations of employees, unions, and other task teams or standing committees. One goal is to create a cadre of champions who are knowledgeable about the design and the reasons behind it and who can help implement it. Another objective is to solicit input periodically from the various stakeholders who will have to implement and live with the design.

Figure 15-3 illustrates the nature of the relationship between a design team and the rest of the organization. The left side shows the connection to the executive group—those within the organi-

Figure 15-3
Bridges Between Design Teams and the Organization

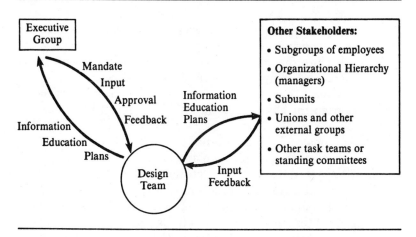

zation or unit having hierarchical power to make final design choices. This group gives the design team its mandate and legitimizes its design efforts. In some cases, for example, designing a new manufacturing plant, the executive group may itself be the initial design team. Generally, however, the design team includes some members of the executive group and other stakeholders. Unless the relationship between the executive group and the design team is well defined, ambiguity will exist about who makes the final design choices and how "official" those decisions are.

Ongoing interaction between the executive group and the design team is essential if the two groups are to move in concert. The executive group can quickly overturn long hours of hard and creative design work at a high cost to the organization in terms of morale and goodwill of the employees. It is incumbent on the design team to keep the executive group fully informed and to get its commitment at key junctures. Designers must "educate" the executive group about the foundation that is being laid and get their input and cooperation on such key issues as values, design criteria, design alternatives, and design choices. The executives, in turn, must commit themselves to learning and responding to the design team and spending the time to become actively committed to the emerging design.

This point often seems paradoxical to both the executive group and the design team. The executive group may be accustomed to reviewing and approving "completed staff work"—projects and programs that have been fully designed and defended. They have turned a project over to a team precisely so it can do the work for them. Once approved, the executive group is used to turning the programs back to the appropriate staff group to implement. However, fundamental organizational change *cannot occur in this manner*. Implementation requires the full and active backing of managers from the chief executive officer on down. Fundamental change can occur only if the executive group is very knowledgeable about the rationale for the design and has bought into its implications for their "part" of the organization and for their own behavior.

At Newtel, the design team at each level in the organization reported its progress (and the problems that were arising) at regular intervals to the appropriate management group. This practice occurred in an interactive format where design team members attended the management meeting or invited the management team to come to its own meetings. In this way, the management group was kept informed and had a chance to ask questions, express concerns, and suggest alternatives. This practice also led to the natural consequence that the design effort became the topic of discussion in management staff meetings, and thus managers became actively involved in thinking about its implications and their role in the change.

The right side of Figure 15-3 illustrates the relationship between the design team and other stakeholders. The purposes of this connection are to get more systematic input and feedback from the various perspectives in the organization, and to inform, educate, and prepare others for the changes that are coming. At key junctures in the design process, design-team members can present information and solicit input from important stakeholders. This relationship can be designed to complement the self-design process. For example, during the diagnostic stage, the design team at Newtel planned focus groups where it presented information to groups of employees about the changes that were occurring in the business environment and solicited input about what organizational changes would be required to adapt to the business changes. Various stakeholder groups were asked to respond to a draft of a value statement, in terms of both their reaction to the values and their thoughts about what it would take for the organization to promote them. After the design criteria were generated, interviews were held with individuals knowledgeable about major parts of the organization to share the criteria and to get their input about what design variables seem especially important in their part of the organization. The labor union, which was represented on design teams at all levels, reported to its constituency at all union meetings.

The essential aspect of the relationship between the design team and the various stakeholders is that it involves two-way communication. Often design teams provide information but do not solicit input or reaction. This practice makes employees feel helpless to get their needs and opinions considered. Alternatively, some design teams solicit input but provide little information in return. This practice leads people to feel that their time has been wasted because they have given input and have no idea how it fits in or what is done with it. Each interaction should educate and inform the stakeholders to enable them to provide maximally useful information. This two-way exchange can enhance the felt need for change in the organization and build advocates for change.

Design teams often hesitate to share information with others in the organization for fear of creating unrealistic expectations too early in the change process. Ironically, if little information is shared, then expectations frequently become more unrealistic because people know there is an effort underway, but do not understand the various stages that it must go through. In addition, they come to see the design team as powerful but secretive, a sentiment that negates the positive benefits of creating a representative design team. Finally, failing to share information does not permit others in the organization to be part of the learning process, and thus makes the implementation process more difficult.

Actively linking others in the organization into the design process is time consuming, but in the end can save time by making the implementation process easier. In addition, the more the organization as a whole comes to understand the need for change, is aware of efforts that are underway, and has had input, the more pressure key organizational decision makers will feel to keep the process moving in a timely way.

Continuity of Design Teams

It is important that there be continuity in the entire self-design process. We recommend that design teams persist throughout the change process. Shifting responsibility mid-stream can cause major discontinuities. For example, we worked with one company where a cross-sectional team designed the parameters of an information system to promote self-management and introduce computerized manufacturing. The design team disbanded when it turned over the broad specifications to the information-systems department for further development and implementation. One year later, there was considerable discontent among the former design-team members, who felt that both the intent and the content of the design were being violated and that the information-systems department had taken their design as input and designed exactly what it pleased. Because the design team no longer existed, it could not oversee the change process and had no base from which to influence what was going on.

The need for a stable design team to ensure that the entire cycle of self-design is enacted properly and to provide continuity throughout does not preclude establishing supplemental teams for various parts of the design process. For example, the creative aspects of designing may best be accomplished by a cross-sectional design team, whereas a top-management team may be required to support implementation. People look to their bosses to find out what is expected of them, and if their bosses are not behind the change, behavior will not change. This practice suggests that existing management teams, such as divisional or departmental staffs, have a key role in the implementation and assessment stage of self-design. They should work closely with the design teams to ensure that the design is implemented and adequately assessed.

Figure 15-4 illustrates one configuration of how responsibility might shift through the various stages of self-design. In our experience, design teams are generally established because of a change in corporate strategy or because organizational changes are required to enact the current strategy in a changed environment. The strategic direction is determined by the executive group, although the strategy-making process is sometimes very participative. The executive group may also determine organizational values before proceeding to the design process; in that case, corporate values become an input to the design team. The valuing stage of self-design thus is split between the top executives and the design team (which may include some executives). The design team interprets and clarifies the values that the executive group has formulated and tries

Figure 15-4
Structure for the Stages of Self-Design

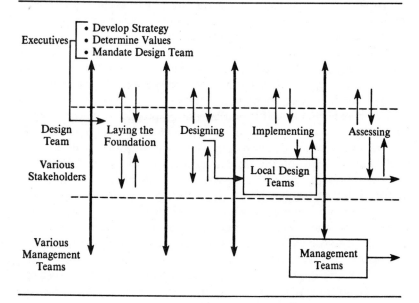

to put them into operation. It engages in a dialogue that helps the executive group refine the values.

In this illustration, the design team is created specially for the design process. In other cases, such as a new plant design, design teams may comprise existing organizational units, starting with the top-management team and cascading downward throughout the entire organization. In Figure 15-4, the design team is a multi-stakeholder group, not an existing unit. We have illustrated this phenomenon by boxing its activities off from the normal hierarchy of the organization. The two-way arrows indicate the need for communication not only between the design team and the regular organizational hierarchy, but also between levels of the hierarchy about the self-design effort. Managers at all levels have to hear from their hierarchical superiors about the nature of the change process, how it relates to them, and what kind of changes will be expected of them. When implementation begins, they have to hear from their bosses that they are responsible for successful implementation in their particular areas. The design team will provide them with information and resources, but it does not have authority to command that anything be done. The design team needs the support of the hierarchy for the change to take place.

Failure to understand this issue has caused many organizations long delays in implementing change. After the design is created, the organization erroneously expects the design team to implement it. In fact, managers will look to their bosses to see if change is expected and if it will be viewed positively, and to see if their bosses are changing their behavior. Thus the design team will have to work closely with and through the organizational hierarchy. The team is responsible for providing resources, tools, and assistance to local units that are trying to change, including helping managers to learn how to manage differently. At Imaginative Systems (Chapter 6), a high-technology company transitioning to an interfunctional teamwork design, managers throughout the organization were asked to report on progress at each staff meeting, where time was spent discussing and sharing ideas about problems that were arising. The design team had developed a team-building process to help each staff develop this way of operating, and provided process assistance to the staff meetings and other resources to help address the problems. It was made clear that responsibility for implementation of the new design lay with line managers, but that they were expected to work closely with the design team.

Summary

Structuring the self-design process is key to its success. The more complex the organization and multifaceted the design, the greater the number of design teams that will be required and the greater the task of coordinating them. Teams should be composed of people who have the requisite variety of perspectives and expertise and who are influential in the organization. Design teams are change agents. They consequently must conduct their activities to create a felt need for change in the organization and to develop a cadre of informed advocates of the forthcoming change. Throughout the self-design cycle, support for and information about the self-design should flow through the organizational hierarchy. This practice is particularly applicable to the implementation phase, where top-to-bottom change and support are required, and line management must be held accountable for implementing the new design in their units.

Design Roles for Large-Scale Change

In large-scale change situations, a great number of people may have special roles in self-design. This section describes several possible roles that may be necessary to manage and carry out such complex organizational change.

The Executive Group

This group, and ultimately the CEO, is responsible for the strategic and institutional leadership of the organization and, consequently, for its design and performance. It cannot turn this responsibility nor accountability over to a design team. The design team operates as an extension of the executive group. It receives its mandate and ongoing input, reactions, and design approval from this group. The executive group must commit sufficient time to be thoroughly familiar with the activities of the design team and to understand what it is approving at each step. In addition, the executive group provides visible leadership throughout the organization in supporting the design team and the design that emerges. It models the new behaviors that are required to enact the design. For example, it will be very difficult for an organization to move to a culture of teamwork if the executive group itself does not operate as a team. Executive-group members must also demonstrate support for self-design and its outcomes through the expectations they establish for those reporting to them and the importance they place on the design activities.

Design Team Members

Each design-team member has the responsibility to learn what is needed to be part of a self-design process and to represent particular perspectives and bring special expertise to the design process. In addition, members keep others in the organization informed about what is happening in the design process and provide feedback to the team about reactions in the organization. They monitor the design process, sense trouble spots, and initiate corrective activity. Although learning occurs throughout the organization, the design team is the catalyst for and the focal point of the learning process.

Design-Team Leaders

Team leaders are key spokespeople for what is happening in the design process. Although active in the team process, they will additionally spend a great deal of time interacting with influential stakeholders to pave the way for the new design and the implementation activities. Leaders of local design teams, such as supervisors of specific organizational units, play the same role in their part of the organization.

Consultants

When consultants are used, they should provide particular expertise either in the content or the process of self-design. They should not tell the team how to design its organization or unit. Consultants can provide valuable learning from previous design experiences with other organizations. The consultant may bring expertise in particular design features that can be helpful in laying the design team's foundation. This wider knowledge and experience complements that of organizational members in their own company and in their discipline. The consultant is appropriately part of a collaborative effort. When the consultant is external to the company, one explicit task should be to transmit his or her expertise to appropriate in-house individuals so that the capacity for self-design becomes built in. Consultants who specialize in job design, for example, should teach several line managers the principles of their trade. Consultants who specialize in the process of change should groom the project manager and/or other internal people to manage change. This procedure should help to provide a cadre of internal individuals skilled in design and change.

Project Manager

The daily planning and managing of resources for self-design in large-scale change settings are often performed by someone in a project-management role. This person will be in charge of planning, scheduling, communicating, and coordinating the multifaceted activities of self-design and the resources assigned to it. The project manager works closely with the design-team leadership. In addition to the project manager, one or more people may provide administrative and coordinative support to the design teams. Some projects require a great deal of training, team building, data collection, report preparation, orientation sessions, and the like. The project manager typically ensures that these things are happening and coordinates the specialized resources required.

The project manager should be, or must quickly become, knowledgeable about organizational change and should provide operational leadership and coordination to the self-design process.

Frequently, the project manager gains expertise by working closely with an external or internal consultant in the early stages of the process. The project manager should define the role as managing the process of self-design, *not* as getting members to agree to what he or she wants to do. This role requires someone skilled at working through others. Because the project manager has no direct hierarchical power over most of the people who have to change their behavior to make the new design work, the basis for effectiveness is expertise, trust, respect, and a broad knowledge of the organization.

Managers

When the new design represents systemic change, all managers will become actively involved in its implementation. The design will not achieve fruition if managers "let it happen" or actively avoid it. All managers have to be helped to be change agents in their work units. They must work cooperatively with design teams, use the resources available, and provide for leadership in their work units. No design team can think of everything. Consequently, managers throughout the organization must encourage and assist their members to devise ways to make the design work. This procedure will require considerable local innovation and modification of the design.

Staff Groups

Systemic change typically involves many staff groups: human resources, finance, information systems, purchasing, and so forth. These groups function to support not only the strategic direction of the company, but also the new design. In some cases, they will provide expertise in the design process. They may also be charged with designing systems needed to make the new design work. Their role is as partners with line managers and other staff groups in the design and implementation process, rather than as defenders of their own systems and practices.

Unions

It is beyond the scope of this book to discuss the intricacies of self-design in unionized settings. We can say, however, that unions are key stakeholders in the change process and must consequently become partners in change. This goal can be achieved by having union representation on design teams and having the union share in communication and implementation activities. This involvement must be authentic not token, or surely it will come back to haunt the organization.

Employees

Employees at all levels of the organization play a key role in self-design. They may be asked to be part of design or implementation teams. They may be asked to give input through surveys, interviews, or focus groups. They will be exposed to the new design through orientations and to new ways of doing things through training. In their own work units, they will be asked to become directly involved in implementing, modifying, and refining the design.

Conclusion

This chapter addresses applications of self-design to large-scale change. In such change efforts involving total organizations and multiple design components, one or more specially created design teams manage the design process for the organization. The teams coordinate the change activities and manage relationships with key stakeholders. The chapter discussed the composition of these teams and how they should relate to the existing organization structure. Possible key roles in the design process involved the executive group, design-team members and leaders, consultants, project manager, managers, staff groups, unions, and employees.

16

Concluding Comments

Organizations exist today in an environment that is changing in fundamental ways and is demanding changes in organizations that go well beyond the status quo. New organizational forms are emerging, and older organizations are having to alter most aspects of their design. These new organizational forms will have to be able to transform themselves through time, as there is no sign that the environment will become more stable any time soon. Continuous improvement and redesign will be characteristics of successful organizations of the future.

Tomorrow's organizations will be learning communities. Their members will be able to try new approaches—learning what works and discarding what does not—and to monitor and change the organization. They will be adept not only at planning and designing change, but also at implementing and refining it.

Successful organizations must deal simultaneously with needs for integration and differentiation. They must establish common direction and uniformity when appropriate and integrate diverse parts of the organization when common action is required. Yet they must also encourage local innovation and diversity as units seek to improve their performance, in some cases becoming self-contained.

We have argued that the organization for today's world must be flexible—it must see design features as temporary. It must be information-rich—creating and maintaining multiple information channels that integrate the efforts of many diverse parts of the organization. Yet it must work toward creating self-contained units that can maximize their own performance. The organization that can address today's challenges must find ways to involve many stakeholders in determining its destiny.

These are heavy prescriptions, full of paradoxes and contradictions. Managing both uniformity and diversity places heavy demands on organizational members for increased communicating, risk-taking, learning, and changing. Organizations must become adept at involving, informing, and gaining commitment from diverse stakeholders, empowering people to do what is necessary to achieve organizational goals, and ensuring that those who contribute share in the rewards.

Self-design is a change strategy appropriate for today's environment. The foundation for this process is periodic updating of knowledge and values and regular assessment of how the organization is doing living up to its values and accomplishing its valued outcomes. Self-design involves ongoing assessment, innovation, and change in order to maintain and improve the organization's effectiveness in its environment. The process involves an action-learning cycle in which new designs are implemented and assessed. Data are collected and the organization learns how to better implement the designs and to modify them when necessary. Through feedback and learning, the organization discovers when it is necessary to cycle back to redesign or even to examine its environment, strategy, and values and to begin the entire self-design cycle anew.

Flexibility of organizational design is inherent in the dynamic and iterative nature of self-design. The self-design process embodies the dual focus on integrating various organizational components while enabling self-contained units to maximize their own performance. The principle of minimal specification implies that gross design guidelines will be created to link various parts of the organization in an overall framework. Within these guidelines each unit can find the design solution that maximizes its own performance. Effective self-design is highly participative. Stakeholders throughout the organization are involved in every part of the process: laying the foundation, designing, implementing, and assessing. Organizations that establish a norm of participation through the self-design process will have made that norm salient for the organization as a whole.

Self-design can be used by the simplest of systems, such as a small work group, or by highly complex corporations, such as multinational firms. The more complex the system, the more elaborate the structure for self-design must be, and the greater the number of design efforts that must occur simultaneously. Self-design must be systemic, with designers recognizing the need for the various features of the organization to be compatible. On the other hand, various units of the organization must be empowered to design themselves. Only when organizationally required should higher organization levels constrain the design choices of lower level units.

The norms of learning, sharing, and empowering that are inherent in self-design are at variance with the culture of traditional bureaucratic organizations. As an organization learns to self-design, it adopts new norms and its culture gradually changes. The task is not insignificant and requires executive leadership that is able to establish a vision as well as model and reinforce new patterns of behavior.

The self-design strategy depicts the patterns of change that we have seen in organizations that have successfully transformed themselves. Sometimes this pattern has been conscious. More frequently, sheer persistence and common sense have led to eventual accomplishment of all the steps. Ever-changing demands from the environment for higher levels of performance have led to almost continuous change efforts.

It is our hope that by spelling out the self-design process and giving examples and choices about how to accomplish the steps, organizational members can better understand the path they must traverse and be more intentional about it. Change is never easy, but perhaps with a roadmap, it is less threatening and chaotic.

References

Andrews, K. 1980. *The Concept of Corporate Strategy*. Homewood, Ill.: Dow-Jones-Irwin.

Argyris, C., R. Putnam, and D. Smith. 1985. *Action Science*. San Francisco: Jossey-Bass.

Argyris, D., and D. Schon. 1978. *Organizational Learning*. Reading, Mass.: Addison-Wesley.

Bateson, G. 1972. *Steps to an Ecology of Mind*. New York: Ballantine.

Beckhard, R. 1988. The executive management of transformational change. In R. Kilmann and T J. Covin (Eds.), *Corporate Transformation*. San Francisco: Jossey-Bass.

Beckhard, R., and R. T. Harris. 1987. *Organizational Transitions. Managing Complex Change,* 2nd ed. Reading, Mass.: Addison-Wesley.

Campbell, D. 1969. Reforms as experiments. *American Psychologist* 24:409–429.

Campbell, J., and R. Campbell (Eds.). 1988. *Productivity in Organizations*. San Francisco: Jossey-Bass.

Campbell, J., M. D. Dunnette, E. E. Lawler, III, and K. E. Weick, Jr. 1970. *Managerial Behavior, Performance and Effectiveness*. New York: McGraw-Hill.

Cook, T., and D. Campbell. 1976. The design and conduct of quasi-experiments and true experiments in field settings. In M.

Dunnette (Ed.), *Handbook of Industrial and Organizational Psychology*. Chicago: Rand-McNally.

Cummings, T. 1978. Self-regulating work groups: A socio-technical synthesis. *Academy of Management Review* 3:625–634.

Cummings, T. (Ed.). 1980. *Systems Theory for Organization Development*. Chichester, England: Wiley.

Cummings, T. 1985. Designing work for productivity and quality of work life. In D. Warrick (Ed.), *Contemporary Organization Development*. Glenview, Ill.: Scott, Foresman.

Cummings, T., and E. Huse. 1989. *Organizational Development and Change*. 4th Ed. St. Paul, Minn.: West.

Cummings, T., and S. A. Mohrman. 1987. Self-designing organizations: Towards implementing quality-of-work-life innovations. In R. Woodman and W. Pasmore (Eds.), *Research in Organizational Change and Development, Vol. 1*. Greenwich, Conn.: JAI Press.

Cummings, T., S. A. Mohrman, A. Mohrman, and G. Ledford. 1985. Organizational design for the future: A collaborative research approach. In E. E. Lawler, III, A. Mohrman, S. Mohrman, G. Ledford, and T. Cummings (Eds.), *Doing Research That Is Useful for Theory and Practice*. San Francisco: Jossey-Bass.

Cummings, T., and E. Molloy. 1977. *Improving Productivity and Quality of Worklife*. New York: Praeger.

Delbecq, A., A. Van de Ven, and D. Gustafson. 1975. *Group Techniques for Program Planning*. Glenwood, Ill.: Scott, Foresman.

Emery, F., and E. Trist. 1965. The causal texture of organizational environments. *Human Relations* 18:21–32.

Galbraith, J. 1973. *Organization Design*. Reading, Mass.: Addison-Wesley.

———. 1977. *Organization Design,* 2nd ed. Reading, Mass.: Addison-Wesley.

Galbraith, J., and R. Kazanjian. 1986. *Strategy Implementation: Structure, Systems and Process*. St. Paul, Minn.: West.

Hackman, J., and G. Oldham. 1980. *Work Redesign*. Reading, Mass.: Addison-Wesley.

Hanna, D. 1988. *Designing Organizations for High Performance.* Reading, Mass.: Addison-Wesley.

Hedberg, B., P. Nystrom, and W. Starbuck. 1976. Camping on seesaws: Prescriptions for a self-designing organization. *Administrative Science Quarterly* 21:41–65.

Jantsch, E. 1975. *Design for Evolution.* New York: George Braziller.

Kanter, R. 1983. *The Change Masters: Innovation for Productivity in the American Corporation.* New York: Simon and Schuster.

Kilmann, R. 1984. *Beyond the Quick Fix: Managing Five Tracks to Organizational Success.* San Francisco: Jossey-Bass.

Kilmann, R., and T. Covin (Eds.). 1988. *Corporate Transformation.* San Francisco: Jossey-Bass.

Kilmann, R., M. J. Saxton, and R. Serpa (Eds.). 1985. *Gaining Control of the Corporate Culture.* San Francisco: Jossey-Bass.

Kotter, J. 1978. *Organizational Dynamics: Diagnosis and Intervention.* Reading, Mass.: Addison-Wesley.

Latham, G., and E. Locke. 1979. Goal setting—A motivational technique that works. *Organizational Dynamics* 7:68–80.

Lawler, E. E., III. 1980. *Pay and Organization Development.* Reading, Mass.: Addison-Wesley.

———., III. 1986. *High Involvement Management.* San Francisco: Jossey-Bass.

Lawler, E. E., III, and S. A. Mohrman. 1985. Quality circles after the fad. *Harvard Business Review* 63(1):64–71.

———. 1987. Quality circles: After the honeymoon. *Organizational Dynamics* Spring:42–54.

Lawler, E. E., III, D. Nadler, and C. Cammann (Eds.). 1980. *Organizational Assessment.* New York: Wiley.

Lewin, K. 1951. *Field Theory in Social Science.* New York: Harper and Row.

McWhinney, W. 1980. Paedogenesis and other modes of design. In T. Cummings (Ed.), *Systems Theory for Organization Development.* Chichester, England: Wiley.

Miles, R., and C. Snow. 1978. *Environmental Strategy and Organization Structure.* New York: McGraw-Hill.

Mintzberg, H. 1979. *The Structuring of Organizations.* Englewood Cliffs, N.J.: Prentice-Hall.

Mitroff, I. 1987. *Business Not as Usual.* San Francisco: Jossey-Bass.

Mohrman, S. A., and T. Cummings. 1983. Implementing quality-of-work-life programs by managers. In R. Ritvo and A. Sargent (Eds.), *The NTL Managers' Handbook.* Arlington, Va.: NTL Institute.

Mohrman, S. A., G. Ledford, E. E. Lawler, and A. Mohrman. 1986. Quality of worklife: Implications for industrial psychology. In C. Cooper (Ed.), *Review of Industrial/Organizational Psychology.* London: Wiley.

Mohrman, A., G. Ledford, S. A. Mohrman, T. Cummings, and E. E. Lawler, III. 1989. *Large-Scale Organizational Change.* San Francisco: Jossey-Bass.

Nadler, D. 1977. *Feedback and Organization Development: Using Data Based Methods.* Reading, Mass.: Addison-Wesley.

————. Managing organizational change: An integrative perspective. *Journal of Applied Behavioral Science* 17:191–211.

Naisbitt, J., and P. Aburdene. 1985. *Re-inventing the Corporation.* New York: Warner Books.

Nunnally, J. 1967. *Psychometric Theory.* New York: McGraw-Hill.

O'Toole, J. 1985. *Vanguard Management.* New York: Doubleday.

Peters, T. 1987. *Thriving on Chaos.* New York: Knopf.

Pinchot, G. 1985. *Intrapreneuring.* New York: Harper and Row.

Porras, J. 1987. *Stream Analysis: A Powerful Way to Diagnose and Manage Organizational Change.* Reading, Mass.: Addison-Wesley.

Rogers, E. 1983. *The Diffusion of Innovations,* 3rd ed. New York: The Free Press.

Schein, E. 1985. *Organizational Culture and Leadership.* San Francisco: Jossey-Bass.

Seashore, S., and E. E. Lawler, III (Eds.). 1983. *Assessing Organizational Change: A Guide to Methods, Measures and Practices.* New York: Wiley.

Seashore, S., E. E. Lawler, III, P. Mirvis, and C. Cammann. 1983. *Assessing Organizational Change.* New York: Wiley.

Taylor, J., and D. Bowers. 1972. *Survey of Organizations: A Machine-Scored Standardized Questionnaire Instrument.* Ann Arbor: Institute for Social Research, The University of Michigan.

Terborg, J., G. Howard, and S. Maxwell. 1982. Evaluating organizational change: A method for assessing alpha, beta, and gamma change. *Academy of Management Review* 7:292–295.

Tichy, N. 1983. *Managing Strategic Change: Technical, Political and Cultural Dynamics.* New York: Wiley.

Tichy, N., and M. A. Devanna. 1986. *The Transformational Leader.* New York: Wiley.

Tichy, N., C. Fombrun, and M. A. Devanna. 1983. Strategic human resource management. *Sloan Management Review* Winter: 47–61.

Tushman, M., W. Newman, and D. Nadler. 1988. Executive leadership and organizational evolution: Managing incremental and discontinuous change. In R. Kilmann and T. J. Covin (Eds.), *Corporate Transformation.* San Francisco: Jossey-Bass.

Van de Ven, A., and D. Ferry. 1980. *Measuring and Assessing Organizations.* New York: Wiley-Interscience.

Walton, R. 1987. *Innovating to Compete: Lessons for Diffusing and Managing Change in the Workplace.* San Francisco: Jossey-Bass.

Waterman, R. 1987. *The Renewal Factor.* Toronto: Bantam.

Weik, K. 1977. Organizational design: Organizations as self-designing systems. *Organizational Dynamics* Autumn.

Weisbord, M. 1987. *Productive Workplaces.* San Francisco: Jossey-Bass.

Zaltman, G., R. Duncan, and J. Holbek. 1973. *Innovations and Organizations.* New York: Wiley.